THE
BURNING BUSH
OF PROSE POETRY

RICKY CLEMONS

PUBLISHED BY FIEDLI PUBLISHING, INC.

ISBN: 978-1-955622-47-9

Published by

Fideli Publishing, Inc.
119 W. Morgan St.
Martinsville, IN 46151
www.FideliPublishing.com

Table of Contents

The Burning Bush
of Prose Poetry

Jesus speaks to us through the burning bush of prose poetry that burns in the hearts of anyone who loves to read poetry about the Lord Jesus Christ.

It was the Lord Jesus Christ who spoke to Moses in the burning bush up on the mountain.

Jesus Christ was God in the burning bush that greatly amazed Moses, who had never seen anything like it.

Jesus speaks to you and me through the burning bush of prose poetry that the holy spirit inspired holy men and women to write about and recite poetry about the love of Jesus Christ.

The burning bush of poetry will burn with the hot flames of prose poetry and rhyming poetry about our Lord and Savior Jesus Christ.

The Lord has given all of His poets the ministry of prose poetry to win souls to Him, who was in the burning bush talking to Moses and telling him to take off his sandals because he was on holy ground.

Every poet of the Lord is on the holy ground of God's heart and gets a burning bush experience when writing poetry about the Lord Jesus Christ, who is the Son of God and God Himself that we don't truly understand.

God has said, "Let Us make man in Our image," and that tells us that Jesus is God too, as well as the Holy Spirit who was in the burning bush.

The burning bush of prose poetry strengthens our faith in Jesus Christ.

The burning bush of prose poetry draws us nearer to Jesus Christ.

The burning bush of prose poetry encourages us to always serve the Lord Jesus Christ.

The burning bush of prose poetry connects us to the supernatural Lord and Savior Jesus Christ.

The burning bush of prose poetry will burn in our minds and cause us to think more thoughts about the Lord Jesus Christ.

The burning bush of prose poetry will purify anyone's heart to believe in Jesus Christ and be saved before it's too late.

The burning bush of prose poetry will burn in our hearts and tell us of God's love of truth.

The burning bush of prose poetry will burn in our minds and show us God's poetry.

The burning bush of prose poetry will burn in our motives and show us God's reasons in poetry.

The burning bush of prose poetry will burn in our prayers and show us God answers in poetry.

The burning bush of prose poetry will burn in our intentions and show us God's purpose for us in poetry.

The burning bush of prose poetry will burn in our nature and show us God's long-suffering for us in poetry.

The burning bush of prose poetry will burn in our trials and show us God's victories for us in poetry.

When Moses heard God speak to him in the burning bush, God's words must have sounded like some prose poetry to Moses who had a supernatural experience telling him to set his people free from slavery because God had not overlooked them.

The burning bush of prose poetry will burn and give us hope in Jesus Christ, who is the creator of prose poetry.

Many poets will use prose poetry in the wrong way to exalt the creature above our creator, the Lord and Savior Jesus Christ.

Should Burn in Us

The holy name of Jesus Christ should burn in our minds and make us think about Him day after day.

The holy name of Jesus Christ should burn on our tongue and make us speak His holy name day after day.

The holy name of Jesus Christ should burn in our eyes when we see Jesus living in our spiritual brothers and sisters.

The holy name of Jesus should burn in our ears when we hear His holy name in a sermon, Bible school lesson and in the lives of anyone who loves to speak His holy name.

The holy name of Jesus Christ should burn in our hands so we do good things in Jesus' holy name.

The holy name of Jesus Christ should burn in our feet, especially when we go to church to worship Him in spirit and in truth.

The holy and precious name of Jesus Christ should burn in our hearts whenever we feel the power of the Holy Spirit moving within us.

The holy name of Jesus Christ should burn in our lives so that we will be a living example to the people of the world who see Jesus in our lives.

The holy name of Jesus Christ should burn in our motives and intentions, which should always be good for our fellow men.
The holy name of Jesus Christ should burn in our actions that are a book people will read whether they like it or not.

The Holy Name of Jesus Christ should burn in us wherever we go so that people will praise His holy name when they hear you and me speak about Him.

Communicate

God knows how to communicate with you and me who He created in His image.

God knows how to communicate with animals.

God communicated with the animals to get them onto Noah's Ark.

God communicated with the snakes to bite many people who were complaining to Moses.

God communicated with the lions to get them to shut their mouths so they would not eat Daniel when he was in the lion's den.

God communicated with the raven birds to get them to feed Elijah some bread.

God communicated to the donkey to warn Balaam to not go down the path where the angel of the Lord would kill him.

God knows how to communicate with all the animals that He created before He created man and woman.

The animals can look at you and me and sense that sin has messed us up and made us sin against God.

God knows how to communicate with everything He created.

The best communicators in this world are no match for God, who can communicate with the storms and calm them down.

God knows how to communicate with you and me, even on our bad days that have no power to keep God from talking to us.

God communicated with two bears and made them maul little children who were harassing Elisha.

God communicated with the wild dogs and made them eat Jezebel.

God surely knows how to communicate with anyone, no matter how sick in the mind and body they may be.

God knows how to communicate with anyone, even an animal.

God always knows how to communicate with you and me, even though we don't always know how to communicate with one another.

You and I can sometimes misunderstand one another and take things the wrong way.

If we take God the wrong way, then we are just downright foolish because God communicates to us all of His truth in love.

God knows how to communicate with you and me in His holy word.

God knows how to communicate with you and me through His son, Jesus Christ.

God knows how to communicate with you and me through His Holy Spirit.

God knows how to communicate with you and me through the animals.

God's communication is all truth, with the seen unseen.

God's communication is infinite with the angels in heaven.

God's greatest communication to all the world is that He spoke through his Son, Jesus Christ, who communicated God's love to all the world because He spoke to sinners with nothing but perfect words all the time.

The prophets of God couldn't do that because they were not without sin.

The Lord is Merciful

One morning, I opened my sliding glass door to let my two little dogs out of the house.

I have a fence around my back yard for my dogs so they can walk and run around.

As I was closing the sliding glass door, I smashed my finger in it.

I felt a lot of pain rushing through my finger and I began to sweat and feel like I would faint.

I prayed to the Lord to ease the pain in my finger.

When the pain eased up some, I let my two little dogs back in the house.

The dogs could sense that I wasn't feeling well, and one of my dogs even sniffed my finder where I was feeling the pain.

I could have closed the door much harder than I did, but the Lord didn't allow me to do that because it might have caused me to have to go to the hospital's emergency room.

I didn't have to go to the hospital because the Lord was merciful and didn't let me hurt myself more than I did.

Thanks to the good Lord, I only had a small bruise on my finger and the pain went away quickly.

No one can tell me that the Lord is not merciful when I've seen for myself that He shows me His mercy.

The Lord Can Use the Least Expected People

The Lord can use the least expected people to build up His kingdom.

The Lord can use the least expected people to follow Him.

The Lord can use the least expected people to praise His holy name.

The Lord can use the least expected people to be His special people.

The Lord can use the least expected people to believe in Him.

The Lord can use the least expected people to trust Him.

The Lord can use the least expected people to bow down and worship Him.

The Lord can use the least expected people to love and obey Him.

The least expected person might be rich.

The least expected person might be a genius.

The least expected person might be very well-educated.

The least expected person might be disabled.

The least expected person might be great.

The least expected person might be poor.

The least expected person might be homeless.

The Lord can use the least expected people, like you and me, to win souls to Him.

The angels probably believed that you and I would be the least expected to be saved in Jesus Christ.

Jesus was least expected in the eyes of the Pharisees and elders and religious leaders who didn't believe that Jesus was the Son of God.

Jesus was least expected to save sinners from their sins in the eyes of the many people who Jesus lived among without sin.

Jesus was least expected to be crucified on the cross.

Jesus was the least expected to reappear in the eyes of his disciples, who were with Jesus for 40 days after Jesus rose from the grave.

Jesus was least expected to get the power over death and the grave in the eyes of the devil, who believed that he had won the victory when Jesus died on the cross, but Jesus rose again with the victory.

No Baby is Born to Hate

No baby is born to hate — a baby has to be taught to hate.

No baby is born to hate — a baby has to be raised up to hate.

No baby can choose to hate, because a baby can't make any choices for oneself.

A baby doesn't know right from wrong, but mature people do.

There are many teenagers who are at a mature age and know right from wrong.

We are who we are taught to be, whether what we're taught is good or bad.

When we are at a mature age, we can choose to do either good or evil to each other.

A baby has no sins to confess and repent to God.

A mature-age man, woman, boy and girl has sins to confess and repent unto God.

A baby can't feel any hate, but a mature person can feel hate and can choose not to hate.

No baby is born to hate anyone, but a baby can grow up to hate because a baby learns hate from the environment a baby grows up in.

There is a spiritual birth that God gives to everyone so that we can be a spiritual baby that grows up to love everyone.

God's spiritual environment will never have a bad effect on spiritual babies who grow up spiritually and who God loves every day.

If a baby is not born to hate, then what about a spiritual babe who can be at a mature age where he or she can choose to love God and his or her neighbors every day.

A baby is pure and innocent to God, who doesn't hold a baby accountable for its sins.

A spiritual baby is pure and innocent to God, who will hold the spiritual adult accountable for living right in Him to set an example for the spiritual babies.

No physical baby is born to hate anyone, but a baby can be influenced to love or hate.

When you and I were babies, we didn't know love or hate but we were influenced by the love and hate of mature people.

No baby knows love or hate, but a baby can be influenced as it grows up and matures, to love or hate.

The Human Heart

The human heart has caused global warming.

The human heart of greedy men has built factories all around the world.

These factories produce a lot of smoke, rising way up in the sky and wearing out the ozone layers that protect us from the dangerous rays of the sun.

The ozone layers are very thin because of the hearts of greedy men who treat money as their god.

The heat from the sun warms up the ocean waters and stirs up hurricanes that can destroy a lot of things on the dry land when the hurricanes surely touch down.

The human heart has caused many diseases to spread all around the world.

The human heart has caused viruses to spread all around the world.

The human heart has caused so much death all around the world.

The human heart is so messed up to God, and a human heart has no power over God to make Him change His holy word.

The human heart can't cause God to lie.

The human heart can't cause God to fail.

The human heart has lied.

The human heart has failed.

The human heart is a global problem every day that God's Son, Jesus Christ, has already solved.

He solved it by giving up His life on the cross to save us from being lost in our sins that are within our human heart.

Jesus is above the human heart and will not condemn the human heart that condemns Him with its sins.

Only Jesus can save the human heart because He always knows how to reach out to the human heart and get it to accept Him with Joy or reject Him with no excuses or explanations that won't make any good sense.

Yesterday, Today and Tomorrow

We had to get through yesterday to get to today.

It was not easy for many people to get through yesterday because it was not a good day for them.

It's truly the Lord who got you and me through yesterday so that we could see today.

Many people died yesterday and won't see today.

We must get through today to see tomorrow.

We know what yesterday brought us, but we don't know what today will bring us.

Today will bring many people sickness and death.
Today will bring many people success.

Today will bring many people some good things in their lives.

Today will bring many people some doubt.

Today will bring many people some depression.

We must get through today to see tomorrow.

You and I can only pray and hope that we will be among those people who will see tomorrow come.

If we see tomorrow, we can surely thank the Lord for blessing us with another day.

The Lord got us through yesterday, that now seems like a dream that fades away for many people who had a hard day yesterday.

Many people didn't know if they would make it through yesterday and they may have believed that they would breathe their last breath.

Many people didn't make it through yesterday and they did breathe their last breath and will not see today.

Today can't promise us that we will see tomorrow, and today will be the last day for many people who will die and not see tomorrow.

You and I can only pray that we won't die today and so that we'll see tomorrow like many other people because tomorrow is meant to be for many to live for Jesus Christ, who gives people a chance to live to see today and tomorrow.

Yesterday, today and tomorrow depend on the Lord to give you and me life to live to do His holy will, which is meant for us to do yesterday, today and tomorrow here on earth where our days are numbered to be short to God.

Yesterday was a great day for many people.

Yesterday was a terrible day for many people.

Yesterday was an uncertain day for many people.

Yesterday was a good day for many people.

Yesterday was a painful day for many people.

Yesterday was a blessed day for many people.

Yesterday was a hopeful day for many people.

Yesterday was the last day to live for many people.

We had to make it through yesterday to see today, and we can only hope and pray that today won't be like yesterday.

Today will be a joyful day for many people.

Today will be a great day for many people.

Today will be a prosperous day for many people.

Today will be a sad day for many people.

Today will be a stressful day too many people.

We must live through today to see tomorrow.

If we live through today, it is because of God's mercy and grace upon us.

Many people will live tomorrow because of God's mercy and grace.

You and I can only pray and hope that we will live tomorrow, but only God can promise that to us.

Yesterday, today and tomorrow is limited to us compared to the Ancient of Days who is God who lives forever and ever beyond our yesterday, today and tomorrow.

Our days are short under the sun, but the Ancient of Days who is God is eternal and will never end beyond yesterday, today and tomorrow that covers over you and me like a rooftop that has a water leak.

The leak will get worse and worse if we don't get it fixed.

Yesterday, today and tomorrow can only be fixed by God, who will fix it when He sends His Son, Jesus Christ, back to this world again to give eternal life to all who are saved in Him.

Yesterday, today and tomorrow will not exist in the eternal life that is all present in God and we will have no days that are numbered when we make it to heaven.

When the Lord Tells Us to Do Something

When the Lord tells us to do something, we must do it.

The Lord will never tell us to do something bad.

When the Lord tells us to do something, it is always a good thing to do.

There are people who do evil things and they believe that the Lord tells them to do those evil things.

The Lord will never tell anyone to do something evil.

When the Lord tells us to do something, it's always for our good and for the good of others.

There are people who will say that the Lord told them to do something wrong, when it was surely the devil who told them to do that wrong thing.

There is no evil thing in the Lord who is good all the time.

The Lord doesn't tempt us to do evil.

It's the devil who tempts us to do evil things.

When the Lord tells us to do something, we will surely be blessed.

When the Lord tells us to do something, nothing will go wrong.

The Lord will never tell us to do something that we can't do.

The devil will tell us to do something that we can't do and make us look bad.

If you know that you can't walk on water, the devil will tell you that you can walk on water.

If you know that you can't walk barefoot on hot coals, the devil will tell you that you can walk barefoot on hot coals.

If you know that you can't walk towards a poisonous snake without getting bit, the devil will tell you that you can walk towards a poisonous snake without getting bit.

The Lord will never tell you and me to do something that we can't do.

The Lord will not tell you to fly a plane when you know that you can't fly a plane.

The Lord will not tell you to swim in the ocean when you know that you can't swim.

The Lord will not tell you to drive a tractor trailer truck when you know that you can't drive a tractor trailer truck.

When the Lord tells us to do something, He knows that we can do it, even if we don't know that we can do it.

If the Lord tells us to do it, we should know that we can.

We Should Not Be Surprised

We should not be surprised by what anyone does.

We should not be surprised by what anyone says.

We should not be surprised by anyone who has a sinful nature to sin against God.

We should not be surprised by anyone in the church sinning, because anyone can fall into sin if they take their eyes off of Jesus Christ.

We should not be surprised by our own sins against God, because we can sin without realizing it.

We should not be surprised by what we say and do, if we don't stay prayed up every day.

We should not be surprised by something bad happening to us.

We should not be surprised if we get sick, because we live in a sinful world where a lot of things can make us sick, even if our health is good.

Our sinful nature should not surprise us, because we were born in sin and that is no surprise to God.

God was not surprised when Lucifer rebelled against Him, and God will not be surprised by who will make it to Heaven and who will go to hell.

You and I shouldn't be surprised if people die in their sins, when we see them living in sin.

You and I should not be surprised if people die being saved in Jesus Christ, when we see them being like Jesus while they are alive.

There are no surprises in God's holy word because it is all truth.

We should not be surprised by what our destiny will be at the end of our lives.

If we love and obey Jesus, we should not be surprised to make it to heaven.

If we are living in the darkness of sin, we should not be surprised about going to hell.

We should not be surprised by anything that is going on in this world.

Every Christian should not be surprised by what sin can do to anyone.

Every Christian should not be surprised by what Jesus can do for anyone who believes in Him day after day.

Surprises are for many people who are living in their sins, because they will be surprised in the second Resurrection.

Could There Be?

Could there be mountains made of pure gold in other worlds?

Could there be oceans made of silver in other worlds?
Could there be cities made of diamonds in other worlds?

There is nothing that God can't do, and God can blow our minds with the things that He creates. Could there be lands made of rubies in other worlds?

God created other worlds that didn't fall into sin.

This world that we live in is the only world that has fallen into sin.

Could there be boundless intelligence in other worlds?
Could there be unlimited technology and other worlds?

We won't know what those other worlds are like until Jesus Christ comes back again and takes us to heaven.

On our way to heaven, we may see those other worlds as we passed by them.

Could there be countless other worlds beyond this sinful world?

Jesus Christ will one day make this world a new world with the New Jerusalem holy city made of precious gemstones.

The streets will be made of pure gold and there will be a sea of glass.

If Jesus can create that, then we just can't imagine how Jesus could have created other worlds that didn't fall into sin.

Those other worlds are so much more advanced than this world.

Sin has caused us to decline.

In this fallen world there are some great cities and great technology that is out of date compared to the cities and technologies in other perfect worlds.

Jesus will one day create this new world to be like the other worlds, and this new world will be the headquarters of other worlds because Jesus will live in the new world with you and me.

Creatures in other worlds will visit us and we will visit other creatures in their worlds.

Could there be other worlds greatly affected by Adam and Eve falling into sin, which may have shaken the heavens?

Worship

No man is worthy to be worshipped, because men die and return to the dust of the earth.

Many kings had many people killed because they didn't bow down and worship them, which comes to show that worship is a very powerful thing.

Only Jesus Christ is a God who was in on the creation of Adam and Eve in the Garden of Eden.

Jesus Christ is the creator of all things.

Jesus is worthy to be worshipped, but even if people don't bow down and worship Him, He won't force anyone to worship Him.

Many kings let their power go to their heads because they wanted to be worshipped, but only God is worthy of this in his Son, Jesus Christ.

There is nothing in this world that deserves to be worshipped.

Not even the angels deserve to be worshipped.

Lucifer wanted to be worshipped in heaven and he is the devil on Earth where he wants to be worshipped.

Many people do worship the devil, who can't give them eternal life after this life is over.

No human being and no other creature is worthy to be worshipped — only Jesus Christ is worthy forever and ever.

Only Jesus Christ deserves to be worshipped because no one else can love you and me better than Jesus can.

Only Jesus Christ deserves to be worshipped because no one else can judge you and me more fairly than Jesus.

Only Jesus Christ deserves to be worshipped because no one else will understand you and me better than Jesus Christ can.

Only Jesus Christ deserves to be worshipped because no one else can help you and me more than Jesus can.

Only Jesus Christ is worthy to be worshipped because no one else can save you and me from our sins.

Only Jesus Christ is worthy to be worshipped because no one else can take you and me to heaven.

Only Jesus Christ is worthy to be worshipped because no one else will always be there for you and me.

Only Jesus Christ is worthy to be worshipped because no one else can give you and me peace of mind better than Jesus can.

Only Jesus Christ is worthy to be worshipped because no one else can heal you and me better than Jesus can.

Nothing in this world is worthy to be worshipped.

This temporary world will one day pass away like it never existed, but Jesus is eternal life to be worshipped above this fallen world.

The Lord Knows All

The Lord knows all that we have done since we were little children.

The Lord knows every good and bad word we have said.

The Lord knows every good and bad thing we have done since we were little children.

We don't know every good and bad word that we've said.

We don't know every good and bad thing that we've done since we were little children.

The Lord winked his eye at our ignorance when we were little children who didn't know a lot of right from wrong.

Our parents were once little children too, and they didn't know a lot of right from wrong then either.

We adults today know a lot of right from wrong.

We have a mature mind, and truly know the choices that we make.

We adults are very aware of what we say and do, whether it be good or evil.

Children can be selfish and not realize they are being selfish.

Adults can be selfish and be proud of being selfish.

The Lord has known all of our minds and hearts since we were little children who were ignorant in a lot of ways.

We went to school to learn things that we had not experienced in our lives.

We were learning to get an education with little experience.

The Lord knows all that we understood and didn't understand in our childhood years.

We did wrong things then, as if it wouldn't catch up with us one day.

The Lord knows all of our childhood innocence and guilt even if we didn't know.

We were once little children with a free will choice, but we didn't truly know what the results of our choices would be.

Being adults today, we have a pretty good idea of the results of the choices that we make.

Our adult maturity has its advantage over childhood immaturity.

The Lord knows all adults' and children's minds and hearts, and parents are held accountable for their children's sins.

Parents are supposed to teach their children right from wrong.

The Lord knows all fathers and mothers, both good and bad.

The Lord knows all teenagers, both innocent and guilty.

The Lord loves us all and judges us fairly.

Knowing Your Holy Word, O Lord

Knowing Your holy word, O Lord, gives me peace of mind.

Knowing Your holy word, O Lord, gives me strength.

Knowing Your holy word, O Lord, comforts me.

Knowing Your holy word, O Lord, energizes me.

Knowing Your holy word, O Lord, heals my mind.

Knowing Your holy word, O Lord, lifts me up when I'm feeling down.

Knowing Your holy word, O Lord, is like good medicine.

Knowing Your holy word, O Lord, brings me back to You when I am going astray.

Knowing Your holy word, O Lord, is the truth to set me free from lies.

Knowing Your holy word, O Lord, secures my life.

Knowing Your holy word, O Lord, lifts me up out of discouragement.

Knowing Your holy word, O Lord, leads me and guides me through my trials.

Knowing Your holy word, O Lord, protects me from the devil's schemes.

Knowing Your holy word, O Lord, revives me.

Knowing Your holy word, O Lord, encourages me to make the right choices.

Knowing Your holy word, O Lord, takes me up and out of nonsense.

Knowing Your holy word, O Lord, keeps me from going down the wrong path.

Knowing Your holy word, O Lord, sets me right when I am wrong.

Knowing Your holy word, O Lord, brightens my day.

Knowing Your holy word, O Lord, gives me a good night's sleep.

Knowing Your holy word, O Lord, lets me know who you are.

Knowing Your holy word, O Lord, lets me know how to live my life.

Knowing Your holy word, O Lord, gives me discernment to know right from wrong.

Nature Will Tell Us

Nature will tell us to do good things that nature does.

Nature will tell us to listen to God, who can talk to us through nature.

Nature will tell us to look at the good things in life that are a blessing from God to us.

Nature will tell us to take good care of ourselves.

Nature will tell us to not worry about anything that God can work out for us.

Nature will tell us to make peace with ourselves and everyone else.

Nature will tell us to listen to our hearts.

Nature will tell us to spend some time with God.

Nature will tell us to hold on to hope in Jesus Christ, who is our Living Hope.

Nature will tell us to not take life for granted.

Nature will tell us to not give up on our dreams.

Nature will tell us to look forward to Jesus Christ coming back one day soon.

Nature will tell us to run away from trouble.

Nature will tell us to believe in Jesus Christ.

Nature will tell us to get to know ourselves and examine ourselves.

Nature will tell us to learn from our mistakes.

Nature will tell us that the grass is not greener on the other side away from God.

Nature will tell us to hold on to Jesus in the storms of life.

Nature will tell us to live our lives unto Jesus Christ, who is the Prince of Peace.

Nature will tell us to look ahead and not look back on our failures.

Nature will tell us to follow Jesus and not follow this sinful world.

Nature will tell us to love the truth.

Nature will tell us to tell the truth.

Nature will tell us to live the truth of God's word.

Nature will tell us that God lives in nature.

Nature will tell us that God doesn't live in our sinful nature.

Nature will tell us that our sinful nature has no peace like nature does.

Nature tells us that our sinful nature brings on death, while nature lives on.

Nature tells us that only Jesus Christ has a divine nature and gained the victory over death.

Nature tells us that its roots are grounded in Jesus Christ.

Nature tells us that it's here for life, when sinful nature is short-lived.

Experiment

There are many children who grow up and leave the church because they want to experiment with the things of the world.

They feel like they are missing out on something, so they turn their backs on the Lord to chase what they are looking for.

Many young people leave the church and will never come back to the Lord.

They want to experiment more and more with the things of the world that will surely cause their souls to be lost.

The young people who do leave the church never really experienced a relationship with Jesus Christ, because having a relationship with Jesus Christ leaves us with no desire to experience the things of the world.

Many young people don't grow up being rooted and grounded in the Lord Jesus Christ.

Many young people, as well as adults, will only go through the motions of being in church but never really have the life-changing experience of knowing the Lord Jesus Christ for themselves.

The best experiment is to have a relationship with Jesus Christ and go through trials for His holy name's sake.

Experimenting with the things of this world will sooner or later take us away from God's purpose for us.

Experimenting with Jesus Christ will give anyone a life-changing experience and lead them to live a holy and righteous life that they will never regret for as long as they live.

We experience what it's like to live in heaven by believing in Jesus Christ and keeping His Commandments.

Experimenting with the things of the world will sooner or later leave us very empty on the inside and we will never be satisfied.

There are many children who grow up and leave the church to get experience with the things of the world, but that's like chasing the wind that no one can catch.

We Can't Live in a Bubble

We can't live in a bubble on this Christian journey.

There are people who won't like us for being a Christian.

We can't live in a bubble on this Christian journey and believe that trouble won't come our way just because we are Christians.

We can't live in a bubble and believe that we won't go through any hardships for Jesus' name sake.

We can't live in a bubble and believe that no one can burst our bubble or discourage us.

We can't live in a bubble that can easily burst as soon as it touches down on something sharp.

There are Christians who want to live in a bubble.

They claim to love Jesus Christ, but they don't want to go through any trials for Jesus' name sake.

There are Christians who want to live in a bubble.

They claim to love Jesus but they don't love all of their brothers and sisters in the church.

We can't live in a bubble when there are people who will lie to you and me.

We can't live in a bubble when there are people who hate you and me.

We can't live in a bubble when there are people who will burst our bubble on this Christian journey.

We can't live our lives like this world loves us.

We can't live our lives like everyone in the church loves us, because everyone in the church is not who they claim to be in the Lord.

We can't live our lives like we won't go through any hardships for Jesus' name sake.

The devil loves to blow bubbles for us to live in, because he knows that if he can cause us to live in a bubble then he has us where he wants us.

Purpose

My pictures on the wall said to me, "My purpose is to hang here and never change."

My chairs and sofas said to me, "My purpose is to let you sit down on me and rest."

My oven said to me, "My purpose is to cook your food."

My refrigerator said to me, "My purpose is to keep your food fresh.'

My dishwasher said to me, "My purpose is to wash your dirty dishes."

My mirror said to me, "My purpose is to let you see how you look."

My TV said to me, "My purpose is to entertain you."

The doors said to me, "Our purpose is to let you in and out of your house."

My clock said to me, "My purpose is to let you know what time it is."

My bed said to me, "My purpose is for you to lay down on me and go to sleep."

My shower said to me, "My purpose is to keep you clean."

My cabinets in my house said to me, "My purpose is to keep your plates, glasses, cups, spoons, knives, forks, pots and pans in order."

The windows in my house said to me, "My purpose is to let you look through me."

My washing machine said to me, "My purpose is to wash your clothes clean."

My dryer said to me, "My purpose is to dry your wet clothes."

The broom said to me, "My purpose is to sweep your floor."

The dustpan said to me, "My purpose is to pick up the trash off of your floor."

My mop said to me, "My purpose is to clean your floor."

The trash cans said to me, "My purpose is to keep your trash in its right place."

The blinds and curtains on my window said to me, "My purpose is to open in the day and close in the night."

My central air unit said to me, "My purpose is to keep you warm in the winter and keep you cool in the summer."

My house said to me, "My purpose is to shelter you."

The fence in my backyard said to me, "My purpose is to keep out Intruders and trespassers."

The closets in my house said to me, "Our purpose is to keep your clothes in their right places."

One day they all got together and asked me what my purpose was and waited to see what I would say.

They already knew my purpose by my actions that they witnessed day after day and night after night.

They knew me very well and saw Jesus Christ in my life every day and every night.

Everything in my house, as well as my dogs, are blessed by the Lord who gives me the purpose of loving Him and keeping His Commandments.

Everything in my house has a purpose to serve me in some kind of way.

God created me in His image and gave me a much greater purpose, which is for me to live my life to serve Him.

Everything in my house has a fixed purpose that is permanent, but I have a free will choice and I choose to fulfill my purpose unto the Lord.

The Lord gave me a much greater purpose for my life than the things in my house, which can't do a thing for the Lord.

Normal or Abnormal

All of those people who were born normal like me are so blessed to live a normal life.

Many people who are normal are not content with their lives.

Many abnormal people would love to be normal from day to day.

Many normal people take being normal for granted, as if they deserve to be normal.

You and I are so blessed by God, who allowed us to be born normal and live a normal life, even though many normal people take their lives for granted and don't see them as blessings.

We normal people should never look down on abnormal people.

We normal people should never believe that we are better than abnormal people.

The good Lord Jesus Christ loves abnormal people like he loves normal people.

Jesus gave up His life on the cross to save abnormal people too.

Whether we are normal or abnormal, Jesus overcame the world to save us from our sins.

What is normal might be abnormal to some people.

What is abnormal might be normal to some people.

Only Jesus Christ was born without sin to be normal all the time.

You and I can think abnormal thoughts.

You and I can say abnormal words.

You and I can do abnormal things because we were born in sin that is abnormal to God.

There are a lot of abnormal things going on in this world from day to day.

We have a lot of abnormal weather.

The people who were born abnormal truly have it hard in their lives.

They are very limited and can't always do normal things.

You and I, who were born normal, can live normal lives and shouldn't be complaining about anything because we can usually bounce back strong in troubled times.

Even if we normal people get sick in our minds, we can usually get well and live a normal life again.

We all live in this world together, whether we're normal or abnormal.

Only God will be the ultimate judge of what is normal and abnormal.

The Spiritual Pain

The spiritual pain that Jesus felt had to have been a lot worse than the physical pain He felt on the cross.

Jesus felt the spiritual pain of being eternally separated from His Heavenly Father when He was in the garden of Gethsemane praying to His heavenly father and giving up His life for our sins.

You and I can't ever imagine the spiritual pain Jesus felt when He was on the cross and said to His Heavenly Father, "Why hast Thou forsaken me?"

Jesus could bear the physical pain of nails being driven into His hands and feet, but He couldn't bear the spiritual pain of being eternally separated from God because He became sin on the cross and that separated Him from His Heavenly Father.

You and I can feel physical pain, and we might feel down in the dumps.

You and I can sin against God, but we might not feel the spiritual pain of being separated from Him.

You and I will never feel the physical and spiritual pain that Jesus Christ, Our Lord and Savior, felt to save us from our sins.

Be About You, O Lord

I want my life to be about You, O Lord, and not about me.

I want to do Your holy Will, O Lord, and not do my will.

I don't want to take anything in my own hands, because I can easily mess things up.

I want to put my life in Your hands, O Lord.

My life is very secure in your Almighty hands every day.

I want my mind to be about you, O Lord.

I don't want to lean to my own thoughts that can easily think about things that are not like You, Lord.

I want my heart to be about you, O Lord.

I don't want my heart to be about me, who can easily feel selfish desires that turn me away from You, my Lord and Savior Jesus Christ.

I want my days to be about you, O Lord.

I don't want my days to be about me, who can easily start my days off on the wrong foot.

I want my existence to be about you, O Lord.

I don't want my existence to be about me, who can easily disturb my own existence by not living my life unto You, my Lord.

I want my all to be about You, O Lord.

I don't want my all to be about me, who can easily fill myself with pride and selfishness that will take me to a falling away from You, my Lord.

I want my eyes to be about You, O Lord, so that I can see that I can only please You by having faith in You.

I don't want my eyes to be about me, who can easily see the things that can distract me away from You, my Lord.

I want my ears to be about You, O Lord, for me to hear Your holy word being preached in my ears.

I don't want my ears to be about me, who can easily hear what is not good for me to hear.

I want my hands to be about You, O Lord, so that I can pick up my Bible and read it day after day.

I want my tongue to be about you, O Lord, so that I can speak Your holy name before everyone.

I want my feet to be about You, O Lord, so that I can walk where You lead me.

I want my actions to be about You, O Lord, so that I can represent You day after day.

Heaven Won't Be Heaven

Heaven won't be heaven if murderers go to heaven.

Heaven won't be heaven if thieves go to heaven.

Heaven won't be heaven if liars go to heaven.

Heaven won't be heaven if fornicators go to heaven.

Heaven won't be heaven if adulterers go to heaven.

Heaven won't be heaven if proud people go to heaven.

Heaven won't be heaven if selfish people go to heaven.

Heaven won't be heaven if prejudiced people go to heaven.

Heaven won't be heaven if violent people go to heaven.

Heaven won't be heaven if covetous people go to heaven.

Heaven won't be heaven if grudge-holding people go to heaven.

God would leave heaven if wicked people go to heaven.

Heaven is for holy people to live in.

Heaven is for righteous people to live in.

Heaven is for people who are saved in Jesus Christ.

Heaven is for righteous people.

Heaven won't be heaven if mean people go to heaven.

Heaven won't be heaven if God wasn't in heaven.

Heaven won't be heaven if Jesus Christ wasn't in heaven.

Heaven won't be heaven if the Holy Spirit wasn't in heaven.

The Holy Spirit can be in heaven and on the Earth at the same time.

Heaven won't be heaven if evil people go to heaven.

Heaven won't be heaven if hateful people go to heaven.

Heaven won't be heaven if foolish people go to heaven.

Heaven won't be heaven if discontent people go to heaven.

Heaven won't be heaven if controlling people go to heaven.

Heaven won't be heaven if judgmental people go to heaven.

Heaven won't be heaven if unfair people go to heaven.

Heaven is for Christian people to live in.

Heaven won't be heaven if intemperate people go to heaven.

Heaven won't be heaven if discriminating people go to heaven.

Heaven won't be heaven if disrespectful people go to heaven.

Heaven is for people who love God.

Heaven is for people who love their neighbors, and that means everybody in this world.

Heaven won't be heaven if mean people go to heaven.

Heaven won't be heaven if pretending people go to heaven.

Heaven won't be heaven if deceiving people go to heaven.

Heaven won't be heaven if the devil could go back to Heaven.

Heaven won't be heaven if scheming people go to heaven.

Heaven is for God-fearing people.

Heaven is for people who believe in Jesus Christ.

Heaven won't be heaven if disobedient people go to heaven.

Better Than

No one can help you to find love better than Jesus Christ.

No one can encourage you better than Jesus Christ.

No one can mend your broken heart better than Jesus Christ.

No one can motivate you better than Jesus Christ.

No one can help you better than Jesus Christ.

No one can heal you better than Jesus Christ.

No one can understand you better than Jesus Christ.

No one can make you happy better than Jesus Christ.

No one can satisfy you better than Jesus Christ.

No one can talk to you better than Jesus Christ.

No one can feel your pain better than Jesus Christ.

No one can change you better than Jesus Christ.

No one can love you better than Jesus Christ.

No one can lift you up better than Jesus Christ.

No one can give you the victory better than Jesus Christ.

No one can give you rest better than Jesus Christ.

No one can give you peace better than Jesus Christ.

No one can make you healthy better than Jesus Christ.

No one can make you intelligent better than Jesus Christ.

No one can make you brilliant better than Jesus Christ

No one can make you genius better than Jesus Christ.

No one can make you educated better than Jesus Christ.

No one make you prosper better than Jesus Christ.

No one can make you wise better than Jesus Christ.

No one can make you vibrant better than Jesus Christ.

No one can make you successful better than Jesus Christ.

No one can make you wealthy better than Jesus Christ.

No one can make you skillful better than Jesus Christ.

No one can make you smile better than Jesus Christ.

No one can make you beautiful better than Jesus Christ.

No one can make you strong better than Jesus Christ.

No one can make you great better than Jesus Christ

If We Want to Stop

If we want to stop eating foods that we shouldn't eat, then sooner or later the Lord will help you to stop if you pray to ask Him to help us to stop.

If we want to stop drinking what we shouldn't drink, then sooner or later the Lord will help us to stop if we pray and ask the Lord to help us to stop drinking what we shouldn't drink.

If we want to stop saying words that we shouldn't say, then sooner or later the Lord will help us to stop saying words that we shouldn't say if we pray and ask the Lord to help us stop.

If we want to stop thinking on things that we shouldn't think on, then sooner or later the Lord will help us to stop thinking on what we shouldn't think on if we pray and ask the Lord to help us to stop thinking on what we shouldn't think on.

If we want to stop doing things that we shouldn't do, then sooner or later the Lord Jesus Christ will help us to stop doing things that we shouldn't do if we pray and ask Him to help us to stop doing things that we shouldn't do.

If we want to stop sinning against the Lord knowingly, then sooner or later the Lord will help us to stop sinning against Him knowingly if we pray and ask Him to help us to stop.

We must keep on praying more than once.

The Lord wants us to be sure about what we ask Him, even though the Lord already knows if we are sure or not about asking Him to help us.

He wants us to be very sure before we ask Him to help us.

We can want to stop doing something and then change our minds about wanting to stop doing things that we shouldn't do.

The Lord won't change his mind about helping us if we don't change our minds about wanting to stop being that carnal minded man and woman.

We must want to stop sinning against the Lord and really mean it.

The Lord knows better than you and me who can say one thing and do another thing.

If we want to stop being selfish, then sooner or later the Lord will help us to stop being selfish if we pray and ask Him to help us to stop being selfish.

We Christians Will Go Through

We Christians will go through some kind of suffering for Jesus' name sake.

We may go through a sickness for Jesus' name sake.

We may go through a bad marriage for Jesus' name sake.

We may go through a job that we don't like for Jesus' name sake.

We may go through being lied to for Jesus' name sake.

We may go through having enemies for Jesus name sake.

We may go through some friends turning their backs on us for Jesus' name sake.

We may go through a heartbreak for Jesus' name sake.

We will go through some kind of suffering for Jesus' name sake.

We all will go through different things for Jesus' name sake.

It's good for our soul's salvation to go through some kind of suffering for Jesus' name sake.

We may go through some hell for Jesus' name sake.

Jesus won't allow us to be tempted more than what we can bear.

Jesus won't put on us more than what we can bear.

We may have to go through some kind of suffering for years for Jesus' name sake.

Our suffering is all about making us strong in the Lord Jesus Christ.

If you and I don't go through some kind of suffering for Jesus' name sake, then we are not on the straight and narrow road.

If you and I don't go through some kind of suffering for Jesus' name sake, then we are only fooling ourselves and thinking that we are Christians when we are not Christians.

If you and I don't go through some kind of suffering for Jesus' name sake, then we are lost in our sins.

Every Christian will go through some kind of suffering for Jesus' name sake, because Jesus Christ Our Lord and Savior suffered and died on the cross to save us from our sins.

Jesus suffered for us, and we must suffer for Him so that He can save us from our sins.

If we are truly living right unto Jesus Christ, we will go through some kind of suffering for Jesus' name sake.

We can't say that we are Christians and not go through some kind of suffering for Jesus' Holy name sake.

If you and I are not going through any kind of suffering for Jesus' name sake, then our works are in vain.

To suffer for Jesus' name sake is to also give up selfish desires.

We can't live for Jesus and live for selfish desires at the same time.

My Brothers and Sisters in the Church

I want to be happy for my brothers and sisters in the church.

I want my brothers and sisters in the church to be happy for me.

When the Lord is blessing my brothers and sisters in the church, I want to rejoice with them.

I want them to rejoice with me too.

I don't want to be playing church and I don't want my spiritual brothers and sisters to be playing church.

I want to love my spiritual brothers and sisters, and I want them to love me.

I want the best for my spiritual brothers and sisters, and I want them to want the best for me.

My brothers and sisters in the church are who I love to be around.

My brothers and sisters in the church are who I love to get advice from.

My brothers and sisters in the church are who I love to share my blessings with.

My brothers and sisters in the church are a gift from God to me.

I don't want to be lost and I don't want my brothers and sisters in the church to be lost.

The Lord truly knows if my spiritual brothers and sisters mean me good and well.

I want to mean all of my brothers and sisters in the church good and well too.

I don't want to wish anything bad to come upon my spiritual brothers and sisters.

I want to love my brothers and sisters in the church.

I want my spiritual brothers and sisters to love me.

I need to love my spiritual brothers and sisters, and I need them to love me too.

If my spiritual brothers and sisters are hurting, I should be hurting with them.

If I am hurting, my spiritual brothers and sisters should be hurting with me.

We are one body in Jesus Christ.

If we feel some pain in our foot it will affect the whole body — the church body of Jesus Christ is the same way.

Real, true brothers and sisters in the church will forgive one another.

Real, true brothers and sisters in the church will love one another all the same.

Real, true brothers and sisters in the church will be patient with one another.

Real, true brothers and sisters in the church will encourage one another.

Real, true brothers and sisters in the church will pray for one another.

Real, true brothers and sisters in the church will tell one another the truth.

I want to be saved in Jesus.

I want my spiritual brothers and sisters to be saved in Jesus.

I want to go to heaven and I want my spiritual brothers and sisters to go to heaven when Jesus Christ comes back again.

You Can't Fool Everybody

You can't fool everybody, because someone will see you for who you truly are.

If you are a good person, some people will truly see that.

If you are a bad person, some people will truly see that.

If you pretend to be who you are not, some people will truly see that.

You can't fool everybody in the church, because some church folks will truly see you for who you are no matter if you are a Pastor, Elder, or Deacon.

You can't fool everybody in this world, because some people will realize you are being deceptive and trying to fool them.

You can't fool everybody, and you surely can't fool the Lord Jesus Christ, who the Pharisees, Elders and religious people could never fool with their trickery and clever words used to try to trip Jesus up in their traps.

You can fool some people and make them believe that you are good, but the Lord can show someone that you have some bad ways that you may not want to change.

You may not want to change your ways of saying things and doing things that might be bad to someone else.

It's always good for you and me to be kind and honest to everybody.

We can't fool everybody and get away with what we should not have said and what we should not have done.

We can say some words and do some things that are not right, and some people may believe that they are right because they don't know any better.

It's the same way in the church, where some people can get fooled by other church folks who seem to be so faithful to the Lord but in reality are so judgmental to others, as if they are perfect without sin.

You can fool some people, but you can't fool everybody inside and outside the church.

Most of all, you and I can never fool God, who knows all of our hearts beyond the words that we say and the actions that we do.

You can fool some people who will be pleased by what you say and do, but you can't fool everybody and make them pleased by what you say and do.

God knows that we can say one thing and change our minds and do another thing that He may not be pleased with.

Just in Time

One day I was driving on the road, and I crossed over the railroad tracks just in time before the railroad lights began to blink red and the railroad rails started to go down.

I was taking my time and driving the speed limit like I very often do.

I drove to another city for my appointment and I only had a few minutes left to get to my appointment as I was driving toward the railroad tracks.

It had crossed my mind that the railroad rails would go down before I could cross over the tracks.

I had no idea that the railroad light would blink as soon as I had crossed over the railroad tracks.

The Lord showed me that He is always just in time to keep anyone and anything from getting in my way, especially when I am on my way to do something good in His holy name.

In the Church for Years and Years

Many people have been in the church for years and years and they are still holding onto some sins they don't want to let go of.

Many church folks don't want to let go of their gossip.

Many church folks don't want to let go of their pride.

Many church folks don't want to let go of their false accusations.

Many people have been in the church for years and years and don't want to let go of their lust.

Many church folks don't want to let go of their adultery.

Many church folks don't want to let go of their gluttony.

Many church folks don't want to let go of their fornication.

Many church folks don't want to let go of their discontent.

Many people have been in the church for years and years and they are still holding on to some sins that they feel good about holding onto.

The Holy Spirit can't transform us if we choose to hold on to our unconfessed and unrepentant sins that we can hold on to for years and years, even in the church.

Jesus Christ Will

The poor will always be around.

God will not lie.

Storms will rage.

Oceans will have waves.

Trees will stand tall.

Mountains will be high.

Rivers will flow.

Snow will melt.

Rain will fall.

The sun will shine.

Stars will sparkle.

Moonlight will glow.

Dogs will bark.

Cats will meow.

Lions will roar.

Leopards will leap.

Snakes will crawl.

Babies will cry.

Women will grow long hair.

Men will have muscles.

Birds will fly.

Wind will blow.

A house will shelter.

The grass will grow.

Food will get rid of hunger.

Water will quench thirst.

Love will get the victory over hate.

Hands will hold.

Ears will hear.

Noses will Breathe.

Mouths will eat.

Feet will walk.

Eyes will see.

Minds will think.

Hearts will feel.
The ground will be under our feet.

Trash will be filthy.

Doors will open and shut.

Windows will open and close.

Fish will swim.

Jesus Christ will save all who believe in Him.

Jesus Christ will never fail.

Jesus Christ will never leave you or forsake you or me.

Jesus Christ will come back again to take all of his children to heaven.

Believe that It's Right

Many people will kill other people and believe that it's the right thing to do.

Many people will rob other people and believe that it's the right thing to do.

Many people will cheat other people and believe that it's the right thing to do.

Many men will rape women and believe that it's the right thing to do.

Many people will abuse children and believe that it's the right thing to do.

Many men will sexually assault children and women and believe that it's the right thing to do.

Sin can truly twist up many people's minds and make them believe that right is wrong and wrong is right.

Many people will fornicate and believe that it's the right thing to do.

Many people will commit adultery and believe that it's the right thing to do.

Many people will tell lies and believe that it's the right thing to do.

Many people are proud and believe that it's the right way to be.

Many people are greedy and believe that's it's the right way to be.

Many people are prejudiced and believe that it's the right way to be.

Many people are hateful and believe that it's the right way to be.

Many people are selfish and believe that it's the right way to be.

People are controlling and believe that it's the right way to be.

Many people don't go to church and believe that it's the right thing to do.

Many people don't believe in Jesus Christ and believe that it's the right way to be.

All Sin is Evil

All sin is evil in God's eyesight, but all sin might not look evil in our eyesight.

God hates all sin, but loves our souls to be saved in His Son, Jesus Christ.

God sees all of our sins but we don't see all of our sins.

We have seen sins and unseen sins that we don't see.

You may see a sin in me that I don't see.

I may see a sin in you that you don't see.

I may say something that sounds right to me, but it might sound wrong to you.

You may say something that might sound right to you, but it might sound wrong to me.

God is the only judge to see that all sin is evil, even when some of our sins may look good and right to you and me.

You and I were born with a sinful nature that will cause our souls to be lost if we don't confess and repent of our seen sins that we see.

Jesus came to this world to save us from our sins because all sin is evil to God.

You and I can make the mistake of not seeing our sins and we can end up being evil in God's eyesight.

We Are Not Safe Anywhere

We are not safe anywhere when a gunman can walk right in the church and gun down people.

A gunman can walk into a supermarket and gun down people.

A gunman can walk into a club and gun down people.

A gunman can walk into a movie theater and gun down people.

A gunman can go to a concert and gun down people.

A gunman can drive in the neighborhood and gun down people.

We are not safe anywhere in this sinful world.

You and I can only pray and hope that the Lord will protect us from a gunman who can show up at any time, anywhere when we least expect it.

We are living in a dangerous world in these last days, and this world will just get worse and worse.

We are not safe anywhere and it's very sad to say that, but it's true and we can see it happening in this world.

These gunmen are the devil's human agents and many of them believe that God told them to kill people.

God doesn't tempt anyone to do anything evil — it's the devil who tempts people to do evil.

We are not safe anywhere and we must stay in prayer without ceasing because that's our only protection against evil.

If God allows us to lose our lives, there is nothing that we can do to stop it.

That's why it's so important to live our lives unto to the Lord Jesus Christ because we don't know when our time will be up.

Are Not on the Right Road

A lot of people go to church, but they are not on the right road that will lead them to Jesus Christ.

A lot of people hold positions in the church, but they are not on the right road that will lead them to Jesus Christ.

A lot of people go to church, and they are on the wide and broad road that leads to destruction.

A lot of people hold office positions in the church and they are on the wide and broad road that leads to destruction.

Just because we go to church, it doesn't mean that we are saved in Jesus Christ.

Just because we may hold office positions in the church, it doesn't mean that we are saved in Jesus Christ.

The Lord always sees our true heart condition, even when going to church doesn't show our true heart condition.

The Lord always sees our true heart condition, even when holding office positions in the church doesn't show our true heart condition.

The devil can go to church and pretend to be a Christian.

A lot of people go to church, but they are not on the right road that will lead them and you and me to believe in Jesus and be saved.

We Don't Always Think Before We Talk

We will very often say something that we don't plan to say.

Many times, we say words on the spur of the moment, and don't think about whether it will offend someone.

We don't always think before we talk, and that may offend someone without us seeing it coming.

We can be careful about what we say, but we may still offend someone who is a sensitive person and takes what you and I say the wrong way.

We all don't always think before we talk and may say something that someone doesn't like.

We can mean people good and well with our words, but someone may still get offended and look at you and me in a bad way.

Some people believe that you and I said something wrong, but they don't see themselves saying something wrong.

We don't always think before we talk, no matter how good and well we mean to be to people.

We can be innocent with no bad motives and still say something wrong to someone before we think about what we're going to say.

Only Jesus Christ always thought before He talked to anyone.

Jesus never said one wrong word to anyone, but His enemies always took Jesus' words the wrong way.

Jesus was perfect and he was still accused of saying something wrong.

There Are

There are many big people who are healthy.

There are many small people who are unhealthy.

There are many good people who are sick.

There are many bad people who are well.

There are many tall people who are stupid.

There are many short people who are clever.
There are many educated people who are foolish.

There are many uneducated people who are wise.

There are many loud people who are nice.

There are many quiet people who are mean.

There are many rich people who are poor spiritually.

There are many poor people who are rich spiritually.

There are many ignorant people who talk a lot.

There are many knowledgeable people who don't talk much.

There are many strong people who are weak spiritually.

There are many weak people who are strong spiritually.
There are many people who are lost in their sins.

There are few people who are saved in Jesus Christ compared to the many people who are lost and will miss out on heaven.

The Beauty About Getting Old

Getting old may be a little frightening to some people.

The beauty about getting old is that we seem to have more wisdom.

We seem to have more experience in life.

We seem to have more patience.

We seem to have more temperance.

We seem to have more understanding.

We seem to be more honest.

We seem to be more trustworthy.

We seem to be more loyal.

We seem to be more careful.

Getting old may be a bad thing to some people.

The beauty about getting old is that we seem to be more mature than the young people.

We seem to be more kind than the young people.

We seem to be more stable than the young people.

It is said that wisdom doesn't come with age.

There are some foolish old people in this world.

The beauty about getting old is that we seem to think and listen before we talk.

The beauty about getting old is that we old Christians seem to be more spiritually mature in the Lord than the young Christians.

Is Busy the Most

The devil is busy the most in the church, because he already has the people of the world where he wants them to be.

The devil doesn't have to mess with the people of the world because they are under his control.

The devil is busy the most in the church, where he loves to cause church folks to not forgive one another.

The devil loves to cause church folks to believe his lies and then spread them in the church.

The devil loves to cause church folks to make trouble against one another.

The devil is busy the most in the church, where he loves to cause church folks to not love one another.

God is busy the most in the church, because God loves to give spiritual gifts to His church folks like you and me.

God loves to be worshipped by His church folks like you and me.

God loves for His church folks to come together and pray to Him.

God is busy the most in the church and encourages His church folks to love and obey Him.

God loves to bring His church folks together on one accord.

God is busy the most in the church, because God loves for His church folks to believe in His Son, Jesus Christ, who is busy up in heaven pleading for our sins before God.

One Day at a Time

All that we can do is to take one day at a time in trusting the Lord.

We can only hope and pray that the Lord will bless us to live through this day.

Many people will say what they will do tomorrow, when today may be their last day to live.

All of today is not promised to us to live if the Lord shuts the door on our lives.

All that we can do is to take one day at a time and live hopefully unto our Lord and Savior Jesus Christ.

Many people don't know that today will be their last day to live.

Many of those people believed that they would live to see tomorrow.

One day at a time is too slow for many people, who make their plans today about what they will do tomorrow.

They don't say if it's the Lord's will I will do this or do that tomorrow.

We can't get ahead of one day at a time.

We can only live in hope, and pray that we will see tomorrow.

God Has No Part Of

Many people will put God into things that God has no part of.

Many people will do bad things and put God into it.

God is good all the time, and God always does good things.

Bad things are from the devil, who God allows to do bad things in this world.

Many people will do wrong things and believe that they will get God's approval.

Many people believe that God is on their side and is going along with them in their disobedience unto Him.

Even in their ignorance, God will not approve of their wrongdoings.

Many church folks put God into things that God has no part of.

God has no part of doing evil things.

God gave us His only begotten Son, Jesus Christ, who lived in this world without sin, even when the Pharisees accused Jesus of doing bad things that Jesus didn't do.

God has no part of anything that we do wrong.

God has no part of any bad words that we say.

God has no part of the bad choices we make.

We will reap what we sow, and God has no part in making our choices for us.

It Always Pays Off Good

It always pays off good to live right unto the Lord.

It will never pay off good to live our lives any kind of way.

It always pays off good to love and obey the Lord.

It will never pay off good to love anyone more than the Lord.

It always pays off good to do the Lord's holy will.

It will never pay off good to do our own will.

It always pays off good to give God all the glory and praise.

It will never pay off good to want the glory and praise for ourselves.

It always pays off good to uplift the Lord's holy name.

It will never pay off good to lift up our own names.

It always pays us good to trust the Lord.

It will never pay off good to put our trust in the creature.

It always pays off good to give God all of our hearts.

It will never pay off good to give all of our hearts to the creature.

The Past

The past has faded away like a dream in the night under the full white moonlight.

The past was alive and did a lot of good things.

The past was alive and did a lot of bad things.
The past is engraved in the minds of many people today.

The past lives in the hearts of many people today.

The past centuries were like a shadow moving across the landscape.

The past decades were like a movie scene that time watched so intense.

The past days were like a moment that passed by.

The past hours were like a bubble that floated in the air.

The past seconds were like a bird that flew away.

The past has nothing to hold onto except the Lord, who the past will answer to with no excuses that the Lord will not listen to.

The Lord will hold the past accountable for its pride that greatly affects the present and the future in many bad ways more than good ways.

Your Chastisement, O Lord

Your chastisement is hard, O Lord, but it is good for my soul to be saved in You.

Your chastisement humbled me down, O Lord, before You and my neighbors.

Your chastisement, O Lord, helps me to wise up.

Your chastisement, O Lord, helps me to not make the same mistakes over and over again.

Your chastisement is hard, O Lord, but it helps me to spiritually mature.

Your chastisement, O Lord, helps me to see that it's not good for me to do my own will.

Your chastisement, O Lord, disciplines me.

Your chastisement is hard, O Lord, but it can add more years to my life.

Your chastisement, O Lord, helps me to think before I say something wrong.

Your chastisement, O Lord, helps me to think before I do something wrong.

Your chastisement is hard, O Lord, but it helps me to make the right choices.

Oh Lord, you chastise those You love, and that is everyone.

Everyone will not learn anything good from Your chastisement and that is a big mistake on their part.

Your chastisement, O Lord, is what I bring upon myself for not doing Your holy will.

There is Nothing that is Too Much for the Lord

There is nothing that is too much for the Lord, who can do anything but fail you and me.

Things can be too much for you and me, who should always call on the Lord to ease our burdens.

Things can be too much for you and me, so we should always trust the Lord to get us through even those spur-of-the-moment things that can get the best of us.

There is nothing too much for the Lord Jesus Christ, who we can call on at anytime, anywhere.

Jesus will get us through our hardships, because they are nothing much to Him and He will move them out of our way.

What seems too much for you and me can be not enough to the Lord, who will show you and me that He is all-powerful.

There is nothing that is too much for the Lord, even when things may be too much for you and me to even consider.

The Chickens and the Eagle

There was an eagle raised in a chicken coop.

The eagle didn't know he could fly because he'd never seen the chickens fly.

One day, he flapped his wings and lifted himself up off the ground.

It felt so good to him to flap his wings and spread them wide.

He began to realize that he was different from the chickens, so the eagle flapped his wings more and more and lifted himself up off the ground.

One day, the eagle looked at the chickens and then looked up in the sky.

He had to decide whether to stay on the ground or flap his wings and fly out of the chicken coop.

The eagle saw the chickens running around on the ground and the eagle decided he'd had enough of that, so he flew out of the chicken coop.

When we get enough of the devil's lies, we must fly to the truth of God's holy word because that is a great place for an eagle Christian to make his or her nest.

Peace of Mind

Having peace of mind is doing the Lord's holy will.

There is no peace of mind in doing our own will.

Doing our own will can sooner or later cause trouble in our minds.

Having peace of mind is from the Lord, who we need to keep our minds focused on every day.

The devil loves to trouble our minds with this world's temporary things that have no peace to give us.

We live in an uncertain world where anything bad can happen at any time of the day and night.

There is no peace in the uncertain things in this troubled world.

Only the Lord can give us peace of mind for loving Him and keeping His Commandments.

Peace of mind from the Lord is a big threat to the devil, who loves to cause chaos in our lives that would be troublesome without the Lord's peace.

That's How Life Is

We normally stay close to the people who we feel close to.

We normally talk to the people we feel comfortable talking to.
That's how life is.

We normally do what we love to do every day.

We normally eat what we love to eat.

We normally drink what we love to drink.

That's how life is.

We normally believe that we are right about what we say.

We normally believe that we do what is right.

That's how life is every day.

We normally think about something.

We normally see what we can see.
We normally hear what we can hear.
We normally smell what we can smell.

We normally feel what we can feel.

We normally sense what we can sense.
That's how life is.

The Lord created us to be normal and do normal things in life.

That's how life is for normal people.

Being not normal is a different thing that we can't judge.

For Being a Christian

Many people will talk bad about you and me for being a Christian.

Many people wouldn't want to be around you and me for being a Christian.

Many people will look down on you and me for being a Christian.

Many people hate you and me for being a Christian.

Many people won't talk to you and me for being a Christian.

Many people will lie about you and me for being a Christian

Many people will make fun of you and me for being a Christian.

You and I will have enemies for being a Christian.

When Jesus Christ lived on earth without sin, He had enemies.

There were people who talked bad about Jesus.
There were people who lied about Jesus.

There were people who hated Jesus.

Every Christian will be hated for Jesus' name sake.

Many people will turn their backs on you and me for being a Christian.

Many people will treat you and me badly for being a Christian.

Many people will tear our good names down for being Christians.

Many people have been killed for being Christians.

Jesus was killed to save us from our sins.

He rose from the grave for you and me to be a Christian and be saved.

Authority and Power

A lot of people love to show off their authority and power over other people.

A lot of people love to show off their authority and power over innocent people who haven't broken the law.

Many police officers love to show off their authority and power, especially over people who don't look like them.

A lot of people in authority love to show off their authority and power to feel good about themselves.

A lot of people will show off their authority and power and bring hardships on innocent people.

The Pharisees, elders and religious leaders showed off their authority and power over people who Jesus Christ didn't show off his authority and power over.

They believed that they had authority and power over Jesus, but they were only fooling themselves and surely not Jesus Christ.

Jesus Christ has authority and power over even death, which couldn't keep Jesus in the grave.

This is Not My Home

This world is not my home because this world loves to give me disappointments.

This world loves to give me grief.

This world loves to give me heartaches.

This world is not my home because this world loves to give me uncertainty.

This world loves to give me unpredictability.

This world loves to give me failures.

This world is not my home because this world loves to give me misfortune.

This world loves to give me stress.

This world loves to give me depression.

This world loves to give me weaknesses.

This world is not my home because this world loves to give me boredom.

This world is not my home because this world loves to give me trouble.

This world loves to give me hatred.

This world loves to give me strife.

This world loves to give me fear.

This world is not my home because this world loves to give me disrespect.

This world loves to give me inequality.

This world loves to give me injustice.

This world loves to give me inferiority.

Heaven is my home, because heaven loves to give me the kingdom of God.

Heaven loves to give me Jesus Christ, who is coming back again.

You Can Go Up and You Can Come Down

You can go up in riches and you can come down in poverty.

Don't get a big head if you get rich.

Don't get a big head if you get a big beautiful house.

Don't get a big head if you get a new car.

Don't get a big head if you get a new truck.

Don't get a big head if you get a good high-paying job.

Don't get a big head if you start a business.

You can go up in prosperity and you can come down and lose what you have.

Don't get a big head if you get a good education.

Don't get a big head if you become famous.

Don't get a big head if you get fame and fortune.

You can go up and get a good name and you can come down and get your name ruined.

The Lord can give you wealth and the Lord can take away your wealth.

Don't get proud and boast about yourself, because the Lord can bring you down to nothing if you don't give Him all the glory and praise.

Real Love is Jesus Christ

Real love is Jesus Christ, who loves you and me more real than we can love ourselves.

Real love is Jesus Christ, who loves us more real than our family.

Real love is Jesus Christ, who loves us more real than our church family.

Real love is Jesus Christ who loves us more real than our pets.

Real love is Jesus Christ who loves us more real than our friends.

Real love is Jesus Christ who loves us more real than our spouses.

Real love is Jesus Christ who loves us more real than our parents.

Real love is Jesus Christ who loves us more real than our grandparents.

Real love is Jesus Christ who loves us more real than anyone in this world.

Real love is Jesus Christ who helps you and me to love Him more real than anyone and anything in this world.

Death is All-Present Around Us

Death is all-present around us because there are so many different ways that we can die.

It's so easy to die because death is all-present around us.

Death is all-present around even animals, which death would love to take down.

We are no match for death because it is very quick to set a death trap for us to fall into.

Jesus Christ, our Lord and Savior, has the power over death and will spare our lives from the horrors of death.

Death is always knocking on our doors asking for us to let it in.

We don't always know that death is at our door.

We can thank our Lord Jesus Christ for giving us a guardian angel to protect us from death.

The angels can protect our pets from death which is something we can't always do.

Jesus Christ, Our Lord, is always ahead of death to spare our Lives so we can see another day.

Death is all-present around us and God is all-present around us to let us know that death can't override Him and make the final decision to end our lives as well as the lives of our pets.

Death can't do more than what God allows it to do.

God has the power to hold back death for you and me to live many more years, if it is in His will.

For Myself

I must have a relationship with Jesus for myself.

No one else can have a relationship with Jesus for me.

I must hold onto Jesus for myself.

No one else can hold onto Jesus for me.

I must confess and repent unto Jesus for myself.

No one else can confess and repent unto Jesus for me.

I must pray to Jesus for myself.

No one else can pray to Jesus for me.

I must pick up my cross and follow Jesus for myself.

No one else can pick up my cross and follow Jesus for me.

I must love and obey Jesus for myself.

No one else can love and obey Jesus for me.

I must believe in Jesus Christ for myself.

No one else can believe in Jesus Christ for me.

I must give Jesus my time for myself.

No one else can give Jesus my time for me.

I must give Jesus my talent for myself.

No one else can give Jesus my talent for me.

I must give Jesus my tithes for myself.

No one else can give Jesus my tithes for me.

I must go through my trials for Jesus' name sake for myself.

No one else can go through my trials for Jesus's name sake for me.

I must make Jesus my choice for myself.

No one else can make Jesus my choice for me.

I must answer to Jesus for myself.

No one else can answer to Jesus for me.

I must be saved in Jesus for myself.

No one else can be saved in Jesus for me.

Many People Will Only

Many people will only respect you if you are great.

Many people will only respect you if you are rich.

Many people will only respect you if you are famous.

Many people will only respect you if you are educated.

We live in a world where many people will show respect of persons.

If you are a doctor, many people will respect you.

If you are a judge, many people will respect you.

If you are a great athlete, many people will respect you.

If you are the President of the United States, many people will respect you.

Many of the religious leaders disrespected Jesus Christ.

They were educated about the laws they broke for not respecting Jesus Christ.

They didn't accept Jesus for being the Son of God.

They disrespected Jesus by calling Him a blasphemer.

Showing respect of persons is of the devil, who disrespected God up in heaven where he had wanted to take God's place on his holy Throne.

Many people are lost in their sins for showing favoritism to certain people, when God loves us all just the same.

More Present in the Country

The holy spirit is more present in the country than the city.

Where there is confusion and trouble going on all the time the holy spirit is not there.

There is more peace in the country than in the city.

We can think better in the country than in the city.

We can see things better in the country than in the city.

The Holy Spirit can speak to us better in the country than in the city.

The Holy Spirit can show us things more clearly in the country than in the city.

We can have a better focus on life in the country than in the city. We feel better in the country than in the city.

The Holy Spirit is more present in the country than in the city every day.

Many people have left city life to live in the country.
We can get more filled with the Holy Spirit in the country than in the city where there are many distractions to take our eyes off of Jesus Christ.

When Jesus lived on earth, He went up on the mountain to pray to His Heavenly Father.

It was quiet and peaceful up on the mountain in the countryside.

The country is where the Holy Spirit loves to dwell out in nature.

The Holy Spirit is more present in the country because the city is made up of many people of the world who do their own will and not God's holy will.

The Holy Sabbath Day of Rest

I thank you, my Lord Jesus Christ, for the holy Sabbath day of rest.

I can rest my mind and body from the ways of this world.

I can spend some special time with you, my Lord.

I can rest from the TV.

I can rest from going to the store.

I can rest from going to restaurants.

I can rest from going to the post office.

I can rest from housework.

I can rest from my appointments.

I can rest my mind from thinking about the things in this world.

I can rest my mind in thinking about you, my Lord Jesus Christ.

The holy Sabbath day of rest is a delightful day for me to give You my full time and worship You, my Lord.

I can rest my mouth from talking about the things in this world.

The holy Sabbath day of rest is a day when I can fully empty myself of me for You, O Lord, to fill me with You who permits me to do my own works six days out of the week.

It Can Be a Lonely Road

It can be a lonely road to deny yourself and pick up your cross and follow Jesus.

It can be a lonely road to do the Lord's will.

It can be a lonely road to give all of your heart to the Lord Jesus Christ.

Many people have said that it's a lonely road to greatness.

It can be a lonely road to be humble unto the Lord.

It can be a lonely road to turn away from the world's wealth for Jesus' name sake.

It can be a lonely road go through trials for Jesus' name sake.

It can be a lonely road to turn away from selfish desires and turn to the Lord Jesus.

It can be a lonely road to walk away from fame and fortune to walk towards Jesus.

It can be a lonely road to let go of worldly friends to be a friend to Jesus Christ.

The lonely road to Jesus is a road of no regrets and no wrongs, for Jesus will save our souls from being lost.

It can be a lonely road to give up the treasures in this world in order to love and obey Jesus, who is the living treasure that no thief can steal away from you and me.

The Things that You Allow Me to Go Through

The things that you allow me to go through, my Lord, strengthen me.

The things that you allow me to go through, my Lord, are for my own good.

The things that you allow me to go through, my Lord, are to help me to be more like You.

The things that you allow me to go through, my Lord, humble me before You.

The things that you allow me to go through, my Lord, are to prepare me to do better things.

The things that you allow me to go through, my Lord, are to make me able to be a witness of You before my neighbors.

The things that you allow me to go through, my Lord, whether they are good or bad are for my soul's salvation.

The things that you allow me to go through, my Lord, are to spiritually mature me so that I can live right unto you, my Lord.

The things that you allow me to go through, my Lord, are to help me to run this race and get my prize of eternal life one day.

Blessings

Don't put blessings above the Lord — blessings are from the Lord Jesus Christ.

Don't worship blessings.

Worship the Lord.

Don't praise blessings.

Praise the Lord.

Don't dwell on blessings.

Dwell on the Lord.

Don't get caught up in blessings.

Get caught up in the Lord.

Blessings are good things from the Lord.

If you are blessed, you can surely thank the Lord.

Blessings can swell up our heads if we don't acknowledge where our blessings come from, which is surely from the Lord.

Blessings can cause us to forget where we come from if we don't give the Lord the glory and the praise.

Blessings can cause us to believe that we are self-made if we don't believe that the Lord made us to be successful.

That won't deteriorate if the Lord is in it.

Blessings can cause us to feel so good, but blessings wouldn't exist without the Lord, which blessings can't take the place of.

The Lord created blessings to give us, who should never take the Lord's blessings for granted, something that we don't deserve.

We should never take the Lord's blessings for our own good choices that can't outdo You, O Lord, in blessing us.

If We Break God's Commandments

If we break God's Commandments, sooner or later it will catch up with us.

If we plan to break God's Commandments, we will quickly regret it in some kind of way.

Breaking God's Commandments is never a good thing to do, no matter how rich you are.

Breaking God's Commandments is never a good thing to do, no matter how educated you are.

Breaking God's Commandments is never a good thing to do, no matter how beautiful you are.

Breaking God's Commandments is never a good thing to do, no matter how good you are.

Breaking God's Commandments is never a good thing to do, no matter how honest you are.

Breaking God's Commandments is never a good thing to do, no matter how cheerful you are.

Breaking God's Commandments is never a good thing to do, no matter how talented you are.

If we break God's Commandments, we break up our own life into the bondage of reaping spiritual pain.

If we break God's Commandments on purpose and make excuses for breaking them, we will displease God who will humble us where it really hurts to show us that He means what He says in His Commandments.

If You Are

If you are living a good life where you live, you are not going to want to move away from where you live.

If you are living well in your own country, you are not going to want to live in another country.

If you are happy in your marriage, you are not going to want to get out of your marriage.

If you're happy on your job, you are not going to want to look for another job.

If you are happy to be who you are, you are not going to want to try to be someone else.

If you are honest, you are not going to try to be dishonest.

If you are trustworthy, you are not going to try to be not trustworthy.

If you are good, you are not going to try to be bad.

If you are free, you are not going to try to be in bondage.

If you are in your right mind, you are not going to try to be insane.

If you are right, you are not going to try to be wrong.

If you are innocent, you are not going to try to be guilty.

If you are a Christian, you are not going to try to be like the devil.

If you are saved, you are not going to try to be lost.

If you are living your life unto Jesus Christ, you are not going to try to live your life being of the world.

Back to the Drawing Board of Reality

We lay down and go to sleep, then we dream all through the night.

Some dreams we remember, and some dreams we don't remember.

Some of those dreams are good and some are not so good.

We wake up to the drawing board of reality and see the same old bed that we sleep in.

We see the same old bedroom.

We are back to the drawing board of reality, where we go through pretty much the same old routine of doing things after we wake up from our dreams.

We see the same old TV when we wake up.

We see the same old hallway when we wake up.

We see the same old stairway when we wake up from our dreams.

We see the same old furniture when we wake up.

We are back to the drawing board of reality when we wake up from our dreams, which are far from reality.

Our dreams are not real, unless the Lord decides to make them real.

When we wake up, we can go back to the drawing board of reality and know that the Lord is real and will answer our prayers.

Back to the drawing board of reality is to love and obey the Lord Jesus Christ, who is forevermore real beyond our greatest dreams that point to Jesus coming back again, which will be like a dream that will come true.

It Doesn't Mean

Just because someone knows the Bible scriptures, it doesn't mean that he or she is saved in Jesus Christ.

Just because someone understands the Bible scriptures, it doesn't mean that he or she is saved in Jesus Christ.

Just because someone is preaching Jesus, it doesn't mean that he or she is saved in Jesus Christ.

Just because someone is teaching about Jesus, it doesn't mean that he or she is saved in Jesus Christ.

Just because someone is singing songs about Jesus, it doesn't mean that he or she is saved in Jesus Christ.

Just because someone goes to church, it doesn't mean that he or she is saved in Jesus Christ.

Just because someone is doing good works in Jesus' name, it doesn't mean that he or she is saved in Jesus Christ.

The devil can appear as an angel of Light.
The devil is not saved in Jesus and will be eternally lost.

To be saved in Jesus is to believe in Jesus Christ.

To believe that Jesus is the son of God.

To believe that Jesus is the creator of all things seen and unseen.

To believe that Jesus is the savior of the world.

To believe that Jesus is the way, truth and life.

To believe that Jesus is the resurrection.

Just because someone talks about Jesus, it doesn't mean that he or she is saved in Jesus Christ.

To be saved in Jesus is to live a renewed life filled with the Holy Spirit.

The Lord Knows How To

The Lord knows how to keep us from getting in debt if we listen to His Holy Spirit advice.

The Lord knows how to look out for us so much better than we can look out for ourselves.

The Lord knows how to protect us on the highway roads that can be dangerous to drive on.

The Lord knows how to protect us wherever we go.

The Lord knows how to get us out of trouble.

The Lord knows how to protect us from harm.

The Lord knows how to encourage us.

The Lord knows how to motivate us.

The Lord knows how to help us.

The Lord knows how to lead us.

The Lord knows how to guide us.

The Lord knows how to comfort us.

The Lord knows how to set us free from anything.

The Lord knows how to cheer us up.

The Lord knows how to give us what we need.

The Lord knows how to open doors for us.

The Lord knows how to protect us from our enemies.

The Lord knows how to give us the strength to keep going on.

The Lord knows how to open our eyes to see the truth.

The Lord knows how to heal us.

The Lord knows how to save us from being lost.

The Lord knows how to give us the victory.

The Lord knows how to move obstacles out of our way.

The Lord knows how to talk to us.

The Lord knows how to help us to live right.

The Lord knows how to support us.

The Lord knows how to be there for us.

Like a Slap in Jesus' Face

If we don't thank Jesus for sparing our lives from death, it's like a slap in Jesus' face.

When we get well from a sickness and don't thank Jesus Christ for making us well, it's like a slap in Jesus' face.

When we achieve things in life and don't give Jesus the glory and praise, it's like a slap in Jesus' face.

When we get out of trouble and don't thank the Lord Jesus Christ, it's like a slap in Jesus' face.

When we go through some hardships and come out safely and don't give the glory and praise to Jesus Christ, it's like a slap in Jesus' face.

When someone helps us and we don't thank the Lord Jesus Christ, it's like a slap in Jesus' face.

If we don't thank Jesus Christ for all that He does for us, it's like a slap in Jesus's face.

If we don't love and obey Jesus Christ, it's like a slap in Jesus' face.

It's a Very Hard Thing

It's a very hard thing to be locked up in prison for something that you didn't do.

It's a very hard thing to lose your mind.

It's a very hard thing to lose innocent casualties in a war that is an ugly thing.

It's a very hard thing to be lied about.

It's a very hard thing to not know where you are going.

It's a very hard thing to lose your loved ones.

It's a very hard thing to be discriminated against.

It's a very hard thing to be attacked.

It's a very hard thing for a friend to turn their back on you when you need encouragement and support.

It's a very hard thing to lose everything you worked hard to get.

It's a very hard thing to get rejected.

It's a very hard thing to get sick and not be able to get well.

It's a very hard thing to be hated for being a Christian.

It was a very hard thing for Jesus Christ to live in this world among sinners.

It was very hard for Jesus Christ to be in the wilderness for 40 days and 40 nights without any food to eat.

It was very hard for Jesus Christ to suffer on the cross for our sins.

Having a Dream

Having a dream is not all about getting rich.

Having a dream is not all about becoming great.

Having a dream is not all about giving up your job.

Having a dream is not all about having your own business.

Having a dream is not all about becoming successful.

There's nothing wrong with not becoming successful.

There's nothing wrong with having a dream, as long as you don't put your dream above the Lord.

Having a dream from the Lord doesn't mean that you and I will get rich.

Having a dream from the Lord doesn't mean that you'll be very successful.

Having a dream from the Lord doesn't mean that you must give up your job.

Having a dream from the Lord doesn't mean that you will have your own business.

Having a dream from the Lord doesn't mean that you and I will become great.

The devil can give you and me a dream that won't always last, but a dream from the Lord will last all of our lives.

When We Think on the Lord.

When we think on the Lord, He will give us inspirational thoughts that will travel through our minds like taking a long trip.

When we think on the Lord, the Lord will take our thoughts on a voyage across the ocean of our minds.

When we think on the Lord, He will take our thoughts through the outer space of our minds to reach the spiritual world of spiritual things.

When we think on the Lord, He will fill our thoughts with the sunshine of good reasoning.

When we think on the Lord, He will open the windows of our thoughts so we can get the fresh air of His wisdom.

When we think on the Lord, He will call the storms of our thoughts.

When we think on the Lord Jesus Christ, He will take our thoughts on the mountaintop of what is real, not Illusion.

When we think on the Lord Jesus Christ, He will set our thoughts free from negativity and take our thoughts to the safe haven of possibility.

I Have a Love for Jesus

I have a love for Jesus because He is the best thing that ever happened to me.

I have a love for Jesus because He is my best friend.

I have a love for Jesus because He is my provider.

I have a love for Jesus because He is my protector.

I have a love for Jesus because He is my greatest dream.

I have a love for Jesus because He is my Lord and Savior.

I have a love for Jesus because He is my redeemer.

I have a love for Jesus because He is my healer.

I have a love for Jesus because He is my strength.

I have a love for Jesus because He is my peace of mind.

I have a love for Jesus because He is my all In all.

I have a love for Jesus because He is my best choice.

I have a love for Jesus because He is my everything.

I have a love for Jesus because He is my God.

Going to Church

Going to church will make us stronger in the Lord, if we go to church to worship the Lord.

Going to church will make us stronger in the Lord, if we go to church to draw closer to the Lord.

Going to church will let us know how much we need the Lord in our lives.

If we go to church just to see who we can see, then we won't feel the presence of the Holy Spirit in the church.

The devil knows that we are going to a good place when we go to church to hear about Jesus Christ.

The devil can go to church to stir up strife in the church.

The devil can go to church to show favoritism in the church.

The devil can go to church, but Jesus Christ is the head of the church and will separate the wheat from the tares in the church.

No matter how much the devil goes to church, the Lord has his faithful and obedient children who truly loves Him.

Going to church for the right reasons will surely please the Lord and He will give us the endurance to hold onto Him when the storms of life drench our souls.

Jesus will dry us off in His warm loving church that the devil can't drench with his lies.

The Beautiful Natural Things to See

The white snowflake is a beautiful natural thing to see.

The rain is a beautiful natural thing to see.

The fog is a beautiful natural thing to see.

The dew is a beautiful natural thing to see.

The hail is a beautiful natural thing to see.

The rainbow is a beautiful natural thing to see.

The sky is a beautiful natural thing to see.

The clouds are a beautiful natural thing to see.

The sunlight is a beautiful natural thing to see.

The moonlight is a beautiful natural thing to see.

The stars are a beautiful natural thing to see.

The day is a beautiful natural thing to see.

The night is a beautiful natural thing to see.

The trees are a beautiful natural thing to see.

The grass is a beautiful natural thing to see.

The flowers are a beautiful natural thing to see.

The mountains are a beautiful natural thing to see.

The valley is a beautiful natural thing to see.

The oceans are a beautiful natural thing to see.

A husband who loves his wife is a beautiful natural thing to see.

Parents who love their children are a beautiful natural thing to see.

A wife who loves her husband is a beautiful natural thing to see.

To love Jesus Christ is a beautiful spiritual thing to see beyond the beautiful natural things to see.

Will Lack in Something

No matter how brilliant people are, they will lack in something.

No matter how genius people are, they will lack in something.

No matter how educated people are, they will lack in something.

No matter how smart people are, they will lack in something.

No matter how talented people are, they will lack in something.

No matter how skillful people are, they will lack in something.

No matter how good people are, they will lack in something.

No matter how successful people are, they will lack in something.

No matter how rich people are, they will lack in something.

No matter how brave people are, they will lack in something.

No matter how victorious people are, they will lack in something. We all will lack in something because of being born in sin.

Only Jesus Christ never lacked in anything when He lived on earth without sin in His flesh.

Which One
Would We Rather Have?

Would we rather have peace of mind or riches and wealth?

Would we rather have love for riches and wealth?
Would we rather have good, sincere friends or riches and wealth?

Which one would we rather have?

Would we rather have joy or riches and wealth?

Would we rather have courage or riches and wealth?

Which one would we rather have?

Which one would we choose?

Would we rather have honesty or riches and wealth?

Would we rather have trust or riches and wealth?

Would we rather have contentment or riches and wealth?

What good are riches and wealth without peace of mind?

What good are riches and wealth without love?

What good are riches and wealth without good, sincere friends?

What good are riches and wealth without joy?

What good are riches and wealth without courage?

What good are riches and wealth without honesty?

What good are riches and wealth without trust?

What good are riches and wealth without contentment?

Which one would we rather have?

Would we rather have riches and wealth or Jesus Christ?

When Jesus Christ comes back again, He will give eternal riches and wealth to you and me if we are saved in Him.

Jesus gave up His eternal riches and wealth to save you and me from our sins.

The Worst Deal in Life

Women who have been raped have got the worst deal in life.

People who have no arms and legs have got the worst deal in life.

Babies born with disabilities have got the worst deal in life.

Mentally ill people have got the worst deal in life.

Blind people have got the worst deal in life.

Deaf people have got the worst deal in life.

Paralyzed people have got the worst deal in life.

People who have cancer have got the worst deal in life.

People who have been abused got the worst deal in life.

Innocent people who have been convicted of a crime have got the worst deal in life.

People who lose their jobs have got the worst deal in life.

Homeless people have got the worst deal in life.

Children who have been molested have got the worst deal in life.

People who have given up hope have the worst deal in life.

Jesus Christ got the worst deal in life to save you and me from our sins.

Jesus got the worst deal in life when you and I got the best deal in life because of Jesus Christ, who redeemed us back to God.

Can Use You and Me

The devil can use you and me in some ways that we don't even know the devil is using us.

We can easily believe that we are so holy and righteous and can't say something wrong or do something wrong.

The devil has been around for thousands of years and he knows where we are weak and how to tempt us to sin against God.

We can sin against God and not even realize it until the Lord shows us that sin.

No one is exempt from the devil, who can use you and me in ways that we don't see.

Judas didn't see how the devil was using him to betray Jesus Christ.

Peter didn't see how the devil was using him to deny Jesus three times.

The devil is trying his best to cause everyone to be lost in sin.

You and I can choose to mean one another good and well, but the devil can use you and me to hold grudges if we don't claim the victory that Jesus gave to us to overcome the devil's temptations.

It Can be Hard to see Yourself

It can be hard to see yourself making a mistake.

It can be hard to see yourself saying something wrong.

You can be hard to see yourself needing to change for the better.

It can be hard to see yourself being selfish.

It can be hard to see yourself needing to be corrected.

It can be hard to see yourself talking too much.

It can be hard to see yourself showing favoritism.

It can be hard to see yourself drifting away from Jesus Christ.

It can be hard to see yourself not being like Jesus Christ.

It can be hard to see yourself being messed up.

Can be hard to see yourself sinning against God.

It can be hard to see your own faults

It can be hard to see your own sins.

It's easy to see someone else's flaws and not as easy to see your own flaws.

It can be hard to see your actions having good or bad effect on others.

We Must Not Laugh at Sin

We must not laugh at sin because sin will play a joke on us and laugh at us.

If people say something stupid, we must not laugh at them.

If people do something stupid, we must not laugh at them.

We can say something stupid, and sin will laugh at us.

We can do something stupid, and sin will laugh at us.

Sin will laugh at us because we have a sinful nature that makes us say something stupid and do something stupid at any time of the day or night.

A lot of people love to joke on sin and laugh at sin.

Many people will laugh at other people's sins, but in the end sin will laugh at their sins.

No one can joke better than sin.

No one can joke more than sin, that jokes on us and laughs really hard at us every time we sin against God.

We must not laugh at people's sins, because it's a sin to laugh at people's sins.

Sin can't laugh at us for loving Jesus and keeping His Commandments.

When People Do You Wrong

When people do you wrong, it can have a bad effect on you.

When people do you wrong, it can be hard to forget it.

When people do you wrong, you can hold onto it for a long time.

When people do you wrong, it can hurt your feelings.

When people do you wrong, it can make you mad.

When people do you wrong, you may hold a grudge for a long time.

When people do you wrong, you may talk about it for a long time.

When people do you wrong, you may try to get revenge.

When people do you wrong, it can stay on your mind for a long time.

When people do you wrong, it may mess up your life.

When people do you wrong, it can cause you to keep your distance from them.

When people do you wrong, it may cause you to shed some tears.

When people do you wrong, it may cause you to do something out of character.

When people do you wrong, you can forgive them.

When Jesus Christ lived here on earth, many people did Jesus wrong.

You and I do Jesus wrong every day in some kind of way.

Jesus will never do you and me wrong, because He wants to save us from our sins.

Beyond Our Choices

The sun will shine beyond our choices.

The full moonlight will glow beyond our choices.

This sky will hover over us beyond our choices.

The wind will blow beyond our choices.

The river will flow beyond our choices.

The birds will fly beyond our choices.

The flowers will bloom beyond our choices.

The rain will fall beyond our choices.

The seasons will change beyond our choices.

The snow will melt beyond our choices.

The fog is thick beyond our choices.

The grass will grow beyond our choices.

God is merciful beyond our choices.

God is good all the time beyond our choices.

God is long-suffering beyond our choices.

God loves us beyond our choices.

God's Son, Jesus Christ, is the way, truth and life beyond our choices.

Jesus Christ died on the cross for our sins beyond our choices.

Jesus Christ is coming back again beyond our choices.

Jesus redeemed us back to God beyond our choices.

People Say that Life is What You Make It

God made life and gave life to us to live it unto Him.

The creator of life is God, who surely can give life and take it away.

You can go down the wrong path, but God can stop you in your tracks and put you on the right path.

God is the maker of life and God will get the last word in, no matter what people say about life or death.

You can make your life bad, but God can turn you around and make your life good.

People say that life is what you make it.

Other people can make your life hard for you to live.

There is nothing that God can't do.

No matter what you make your life to be, God can override it.

Job didn't want his life to be hard.

God allowed the devil to make Job's life hard so that Job could show his wife and friends that he would be faithful to God even when faced with hardships.

Job also showed the devil that he would be faithful to God no matter what hardships he faced.

A Long Way to Go

When it comes to You, O Lord, I will always have a long way to go.

I have a long way to go to truly love You, my Lord.

I have a long way to go to truly love my neighbors.

I have a long way to go to truly trust You, my lord.

I have a long way to go to truly obey You, my Lord.

I have a long way to go to truly love my brothers and sisters in the church.

When it comes to you, my Lord and Savior Jesus Christ, I have a long way to go to be more like You.

Oh Lord, you have already brought me from a long way and when it comes to you I still have a long way to go to live my life unto You.

I have a long way to go, O Lord, to give You all of my heart.

I have a long way to go, O Lord, to give You all of my mind.

I have a long way to go, O Lord, to give You my best.

When it comes to you, my Lord and Savior Jesus Christ, I will have a long way to go even if I make it to heaven where I will still have so much more to learn about You, my Lord.

I Can Always Be Sure About

I can always be sure about Jesus Christ never leaving me or forsaking me.

I can't always be sure about what people will say and do.

I can always be sure about Jesus Christ never failing me.

I can't always be sure about what I will say and do.

I can always be sure about Jesus Christ bringing me safely through my trials.

I can't always be sure about this world.

I can always be sure about Jesus Christ giving me the victory.

I can't always be sure about my life.

I can always be sure about Jesus Christ loving me.

I can't always be sure about people loving me.

I can always be sure about Jesus Christ being faithful to me.

I can't always be sure about my health.

I can always be sure about Jesus Christ being there for me.

I can't always be sure about anyone in this world.

I can always be sure about Jesus Christ saving me from being lost in my sins.

People Need to Know the Truth

Whether they're straight or gay, people need to know the truth of God›s holy word.

Whether they're straight or bisexual, people need to know the truth of God's holy word.

Whether they're straight or transgender, people need to know the truth of God's holy word. Whether they're straight or lesbian, people need to know the truth of God's holy word.

Whether they're rich or poor, people need to know the truth of God's holy word.

Whether they're educated or not educated, people need to know the truth of God's holy word. Whether they're married or single, people need to know the truth of God's holy word.

Whether they're good or bad, people need to know the truth about God's holy word.

Whether they're tall or short, people need to know the truth of God's holy word.

Whether they're big or small, people need to know the truth of God's holy word.

Whether they're strong or weak, people need to know the truth of God's holy word.

Whether they're old or young, people need to know the truth of God's holy word.

Whether they're male or female, people need to know the truth of God's holy word.

God's holy word is for all people to know so they can be set free from the devil's lies.

It Was Beyond Realistic

We are so used to depending on what is realistic to us.

We tend to trust the realistic more than the supernatural.

It was beyond realistic that God parted the Red Sea.

It was beyond realistic that God made the Jericho walls fall down.

God is a supernatural God, beyond our realistic ways of living our lives from day today.

We must live by faith in the Lord and not live by the reality that we see.

We can't put our faith in reality, because reality is very limited when compared to the supernatural.

It was beyond realistic that Jesus Christ fed thousands of people with a little bit of bread and fish.

It was beyond realistic that Jesus cast out demons from people.

It was beyond realistic that Jesus made the lame walk again.

It was beyond realistic that Jesus opened the eyes of the blind.

Jesus did supernatural things in the eyes of many people who depended on realistic things to live their lives by.

It's so easy for us to depend on what is realistic to us and believe that we can solve our problems on our own.

It was beyond realistic that Jesus walked on water and calmed the storm that His disciples were so afraid of.

It's So Much Better

It's always good to love yourself, but it is so much better to love Jesus Christ more than loving yourself.

No matter how much you love yourself, you don't know all of your heart that Jesus knows every day.

Jesus wants you to love yourself, but not love yourself more than you love Him because He helps you to love yourself.

You can't love yourself without Jesus helping you to love yourself.

If you don't love Jesus Christ, then how can you truly love yourself when love comes from the Lord Jesus Christ, who is God's beloved Son.

No matter how much you love yourself, you can't cleanse yourself of your sins.

No matter how much you love yourself, you can save yourself from being lost in your sins.

Only Jesus' love for you can cleanse you of your sins.

Only Jesus' love for you can save you from your sins.

It is so much better to love Jesus more than you love yourself, because you can't love yourself if you don't love Jesus who is the love of God.

Live Their Lives

A lot of people live their lives to use people.

A lot of people live their lives to control people.

A lot of people live their lives to kill people.

A lot of people live their lives to hurt people.

A lot of people live their lives to cheat people.

A lot of people live their lives to deceive people.

A lot of people live their lives to give people a bad name.

A lot of people live their lives to lie to people.

A lot of people live their lives to trap people.

A lot of people live their lives to talk bad about people.

A lot of people live their lives to treat people bad.

A lot of people live their lives to look down on people.

A lot of people live their lives to put people down.

A lot of people live their lives to ruin people.

A lot of people live their lives to hate people.

A lot of people live their lives to blame God for their own mistakes.

A lot of people live their lives to not believe in Jesus Christ.

A lot of people live their lives to be lost in their sins.

Assemble Ourselves Together

The Lord says for us to assemble ourselves together in the church to worship Him and give Him all the glory and praise.

When we assemble ourselves together, we get more and more strength in the Lord Jesus Christ.

When we assemble ourselves together we will sooner or later get to know one another.

We will find out that we have some things in common when we assemble ourselves together.

We will get closer to the Lord when we assemble ourselves together in the church.

When we assemble ourselves together in the church, sooner or later we will love one another more and more.

We will get used to being around one another and feel comfortable around one another.

When we assemble ourselves together in the church, we will get more power of the Holy Spirit.

Our prayers will be more effective when we assemble ourselves together in the church.

When we assemble ourselves together in the church, we will get more determination to keep on holding onto the Lord Jesus Christ, who is the head of the church and the reason for us to assemble ourselves together in the church.

Many People Will

Many people will say that they are a Christian, but they don't want to stop speaking words that are not like Jesus.

Many people will say that they are a Christian, but they don't want to stop doing things that are not like Jesus.

Many people will believe that they are a Christian, but they don't want to stop being like the devil.

Being a Christian is being like Jesus Christ.

Many people want other people to believe that they are a Christian, but they don't want to accept the truth that other people tell them about themselves.

Many people will say that they are a Christian, but they don't want to change for the better and make Him prominent in their lives.

Many people will believe that they are a Christian, but they don't have the Holy Spirit living in them.

Many people will say that they are a Christian, but they don't act like they are a Christian.

Many people want you and me to believe that they are a Christian, but they will show you and me that they are of the world.

Many people will go through the motions of looking like a Christian, but they don't love you and me like Jesus, who loves everyone.

We Christians are Human Too

We Christians are human too.

We Christians will shed some tears over the death of loved ones, but we know what it means to pray to the Lord for strength.

We Christians are human too.

We Christians will not always say the right words, but we know what it means to lean on God and believe His every word.

We Christians are human too.

We Christians will not always do everything right, but we know what it means to do the Lord's holy will and not our own will.

We Christians are human too.

We Christians will get weak sometimes, but we Christians know what it means to hold onto the Lord in our times of weakness.

We Christians are human too.

We Christians will get discouraged sometimes, but we Christians know what it means to be encouraged in the Lord.

We Christians are human too.

We Christians will make some mistakes, but we know what it means to confess and repent of our sins unto the Lord Jesus Christ, who was human without sin.

If We Don't Go to Church

How can we be like Jesus Christ if we don't go to church?

If we don't go to church, our faith won't grow in Jesus Christ.

If we don't go to church, we will get weak in our faith.

If we don't go to church, we won't have much strength in the Lord Jesus Christ.

If we don't go to church, we won't have a strong relationship with Jesus Christ.

If we don't go to church, we won't get to know our spiritual brothers and sisters in the Lord Jesus Christ.

If we don't go to church, we will sooner or later stray away from Jesus Christ.

If we don't go to church, we will sooner or later regret it.

If we don't go to church, we won't have a spiritual life.

How can we be a Christian if we stay home and don't go to church?

How can we say that we love Jesus Christ if we don't go to church to worship the Lord with our brothers and sisters in the Lord?

Jesus Christ is the head of the church.

If we can go to church but we choose not to go, how can we draw closer to Jesus Christ?

If we don't go to church, how can we get filled with the Holy Spirit?

The Heart Can

The heart can love deeply to move away in fear and mistrust that disturbs the heart.

The heart can hurt deeply and grieve for many days.

The heart can forgive deeply and move beyond the pain.

The heart can feel deeply and cast out reasoning.

The heart can change deeply and be so misunderstood.

The heart can believe deeply enough to move mountains.

The heart can deceive deeply and camouflage the truth.

The heart can understand deeply and draw out what is certain.

The heart can be burdened deeply and give up on hope.

The heart can misunderstand deeply and that can be troublesome.

The heart can be deeply wicked enough to start a war.

The heart can disobey God deeply enough to be lost in sin.

The heart can love Jesus Christ deeply and be His living church every day of the week.

What Can I?

What questions can I ask that the Lord hasn't already answered?

What can I see that the Lord hasn't already seen?

What can I hear that the Lord hasn't already heard?

What good things can I say that the Lord hasn't already said?

Where can I go that the Lord hasn't already been?

What can I know that the Lord doesn't already know?

What good can I do that the Lord hasn't already done?

The Lord was around before the heavens existed.

The Lord was around before the angels existed.

The Lord was around before this world existed.

The Lord was around before you and I existed.

What good things can I learn that the Lord hasn't already taught?

The Straight, Hard Truth

Many people can't handle the straight, hard truth, especially the truth of God's holy word.

When we Christians speak the truth of God's holy word, we must be careful about how we speak the truth to others who don't know the truth of God's holy word like you and me.

Many people can't handle the straight, hard truth because they are not strong enough to take it into their hearts.

We Christians must be very careful about how we tell the truth of God's holy word to others who have misunderstood God's holy word and use it in the wrong way.

Many people can't handle the straight, hard truth of God's holy word because they don't search the Bible scriptures for themselves so they can learn the straight, hard truth.

The straight, hard truth has pushed many people away from the Lord Jesus Christ because some Christian speak the truth with no soft spoken words of love.

God Created Other Worlds

God created other worlds that didn't sin against Him.

The devil tried to tempt those other worlds to sin against God, but he failed to do so.

In the book of Job there were representatives from other worlds who faced God.

The devil represents this world because Adam gave up his dominion over this world to the devil when he sinned against God in the Garden of Eden.

Those other worlds are filled with sinless creatures who obeyed God when the devil tried to tempt them to sin against God.

Those other worlds' technologies are forever more advanced than this sinful world's technology that can cause many people to lose more than they gain from it.

Those perfect creatures in other worlds can see and talk to the heavenly angels face-to-face.

They can see and talk to our Lord Jesus Christ face-to-face.

This world is very limited and we don't even know when an angel from heaven is present in our eyesight.

God created other worlds that you and I will one day visit if we are saved in Jesus Christ, who is coming back again to take us to heaven and to those other worlds.

Only Jesus Can Give Me Joy

Money will not give me joy.

Only Jesus can give me joy that can be unspeakable.

Money can come and money can go.

Food will not give me joy.

Only Jesus can give me joy.

Food can cause me to become overweight.

Clothes will not give me joy.

Only Jesus can give me joy.

Clothes can fade.

My car will not give me joy.

Only Jesus can give me joy.

My car can break down.

My house will not give me joy.

Only Jesus can give me joy.

My house can need repair work.

My health will not give me joy.

Only Jesus can give me joy.

My health can go bad.

Education will not give me joy.

Only Jesus can give me joy.

Education can deteriorate into dementia.

Joy is from the Lord Jesus Christ, who can give us joy to last all through our trials that can come upon us and won't get us down if we keep our faith in Jesus to have unspeakable joy.

Don't Worry About

If someone asks you for help, don't worry about whether he or she is lying to you.

If you can help people, then help them without asking any questions.

If they are lying to you, God will deal with them.

Don't worry about someone lying, because he or she could be telling the truth about their bad situations.

There are truly some good people in this world who will be honest with you and me.

Don't worry about someone who you believe is trying to deceive you in some kind of way.

Help people if you can help them and let the Lord work on their hearts if they are being dishonest.

Don't worry about anything people do.

Don't worry about what people tell you.

God won't allow the devil to tempt you with more than what you can bear if you love Him and keep His Commandments.
Don't worry about the bad things people have done to you, just be thankful that the Lord let you live through them.

Don't worry about what you can't change.

Put your trust in the Lord, who can make the impossible possible in your life and my life.

Don't worry about temporary things that are not more valuable than your soul's salvation.

Sooner or Later
the Lord Will Show You

Sooner or later the Lord will show you if someone is telling you the truth or telling you a lie.

The Lord sees all and the Lord knows all, and sooner or later He will show you and me the truth about people.

If you and I have a relationship with the Lord Jesus Christ, we will make good choices that will sooner or later pay off really well.

Sooner or later a bad man or woman will mess up on what he or she plans to do.

Sooner or later people will get caught up in their lies.

Sooner or later the Lord will show you some real true colors.

If you and I fall down into sin, sooner or later the Lord will help us to get back up out of that sin if we confess and repent of those sins unto the Lord.

Sooner or later the Lord will show you and me how much He will bless us if we love Him and obey His holy law.

Sooner or later the Lord will show you and me who our real friends are.

You and I will fall short of the glory of God, but sooner or later the Lord God will lift us up out of the furnace fire of life if we deny ourselves and pick up our crosses and follow Him beyond the sooner or later.

You and I can get deceived by someone, but sooner or later the Lord will show you and me that life, health and strength are the real true wealth that will get us back up on our feet so we can start over again.

The sooner or laters in life are in the Lord the Almighty's hands, because the Lord knows all who will be sooner or later saved or lost.

The Lord is My Strength

The Lord is my strength to get me through anything I go through in my life.

I don't trust my strength, because it will fail me.

My strength is weak compared to the Lord, who is my strength and keeps me going strong day after day.

My strength is no defense against depression.

My strength is no defense against worry.

My strength is no defense against stress.

The Lord is my strength against trouble.

The Lord is my strength against depression.

The Lord is my strength against worry.
The Lord is my strength against stress.

My strength is no defense against fears.

My strength is no defense against injustice.

The Lord is my strength against prejudice.

The Lord is my strength against hatred.

The Lord is my strength against injustice.

My strength is no defense against sickness.

My strength is no defense against the unknown.

My strength is no defense against the unpredictable.

My strength is no defense against the uncertain.

The Lord is my strength against fear.

The Lord is my strength against vulnerability.

The Lord is my strength against lies.

The Lord is my strength against pain.

The Lord is my strength against myself.

The Lord is my strength against anyone and anything that is not pleasing to the Lord.

The Lord Will Protect His Children

The Lord will protect his children from falling into traps that evil people love to set up.

The devil has his human agents everywhere in this world who try to cause you and me to fall into his traps.

If you and I pray without ceasing to the Lord, He will protect us, even in many ways we don't see.

You and I don't always see the devil coming our way trying to destroy us, but the Lord sees all things and the devil will never get by Him with his evil deeds.

The Lord will protect his children who have stayed up in prayer and are obedient unto Him day after day and night after night.

The devil has his human agents who love to try to cause you and me and all of God's children to fall into their evil traps that they are proud to set up.

The Lord is not slack in protecting you and me, because the Lord Jesus Christ is always on time to send His angels to protect us.

You and I can never protect ourselves better than the Lord can.

The Lord will show us His protection so crystal clear if we love Him and keep His Commandments day after day.

Broken

We are all broken human beings because of being born with a sinful nature to sin against God.

We all are broken in some kind of way even though we may not see it.

Many people are broken because they are greedy for worldly gain.

Many people are being broken in lust.

Many people are broken because they tell lies.

Many people are broken because they kill people.

Many people are broken by pride.

Many people are broken by envy.

Many people are broken by hate.

Many people are broken because they want control over others.

Many people are broken by self-pity.

Many people are broken by unforgiveness.

Many people are broken by hurting people.

Many people are broken by using people.

The Lord Jesus Christ can fix broken people, if they trust Him to fix them.

Jesus gave up His life on the cross to save us from our broken sins.

Jesus got all broken up on the cross that he died on.

Jesus rose from the grave to fix us all up from our brokenness.

We are broken human beings.

Only Jesus can fix us like we were never broken.

Love To

Many people love to be ignorant.

Many people love to tell lies.

Many people love to fight.

Many people love to quarrel.

Many people love to fornicate.

Many people love to commit adultery.

Many people love to cheat.

Many people love to be proud.

Many people love to lust.

Many people love to do evil.

Many people love to gossip.

Many people love to be abusive.

Many people love to put other people down.

Many people love discrimination and inequality.

Many people love to boast.

Many people love to joke.

Many people love to eat.

Many people love to drink alcohol.

Many people love to smoke.

Many people love to kill.

Many people love to hurt other people.

Many people love to hate.

Many people love to judge other people.

Many people love to envy other people.

Many people love to be prejudiced.

Many people love injustice.

Many people love to riot.

A few people love to do good.

A few people love to deny themselves and pick up their crosses and follow Jesus.

A few people love to believe in Jesus Christ.

A few people love to keep God's Ten Commandments.

A few people love to work out their own soul's salvation.

A few people love to be saved in Jesus Christ.

Just By

Just by looking at people you don't know what they've been through.

Just by looking at people you don't know what they are going through.

Just by looking at people you don't know how they really feel.

Just by looking at people you don't know what they are thinking about.

Just by looking at people you don't know what they will say.

Just by looking at people you don't know what they will do.

Just by talking to people you don't know if they really mean what they say.

Just by talking to people you don't know what they will say next.

Just by talking to people you don't know if they are telling you the truth.

Just by talking to people you don't know if they're leaving out something that you should know about.

Just by talking to the Lord you don't know if the Lord will answer you right away.

Just by having a relationship with the Lord, you don't know if the Lord will test your faith in Him like He tested Job.

Speaking the Right Words

Speaking the right words can surely get rid of anger.

Speaking the right words can soothe a broken heart.
Speaking the right words can surely ease a troubled mind.

Speaking the right words can surely give someone hope.

Speaking the right words can surely give someone peace of mind.

Speaking the right words can surely build someone up.

Speaking the right words can surely strengthen someone.

Speaking the right words can surely help some go the extra mile.

Speaking the right words can surely encourage someone.

Speaking the right words can surely change someone's mind.

Speaking the right words can surely get attention.

Speaking the right words can surely warm up a cold heart.

Speaking the right words can surely help someone to get a good night's sleep.

Speaking the right words can surely help someone wise up.

Speaking the right words can surely spread around.

Speaking the right words can surely save someone's life.

Speaking the right words can surely go a long way.

Speaking the right words can surely please the Lord.

It's the Lord

It's the Lord who gives us beautiful words to express from our hearts.

Beauty comes from the Lord, who created all things beautiful in the beginning of time.

It's the Lord who created the heavens so very beautiful that you and I can only imagine but the angels know.

It's the Lord who created all the angels and gave them beauty for His great glory.

Living a Christian life is a beautiful life to live every day.

The beauty of a Christian life will never get old or wrinkled.

It's the Lord who gives every Christian spiritual, ageless beauty for doing His holy will that is more beautiful than any external beauty.

The Lord didn't create an ugly world, but the devil has made things look ugly to other worlds that have never fallen into sin.

Jesus Christ will create a new, beautiful world for you and me to live in with our new immortal and beautiful body that Jesus will give to us for being saved in Him.

Some Church Folks Believe

Some church folks believe that the church is all about their ministry and them shining in the spotlight.

Some church folks only love to talk about their ministry, as if they are the only ones to have a ministry in the church.

The Lord has given everyone a ministry in the church to help build up the church with new believers in Jesus Christ, our Lord and Savior.

The church is not about you and it is not about me who can't cleanse people of their sins and can't save people from their sins.

Our ministry is to spread the Gospel of Jesus Christ in a sermon, song, poem, Bible school lesson, and most of all through our actions about Jesus.

Some church folks love to get the glory and praise that only Jesus Christ is worthy to get in the church.

My ministry and your ministry is not about me and you who were born in this world with nothing and will leave this world with nothing except to hopefully be saved in Jesus Christ.

Some church folks believe that the church cannot be victorious without them leading in service.

Some church folks are self-centered and believe that no one else can see it spreading like wildfire in the church.

Some church folks believe that they are the only ones who have favor with God and they want to judge people without having the slightest clue about their prayers that may be very sincere to God.

Some church folks believe that they are a mediator in the church and without them you and I can't come to the Lord through our own prayers.

Wonderfully Made

God wonderfully made every human being for His great pleasure that is eternal beyond the pleasures in this fallen world.

God wonderfully made every human being, but sin is from the devil who brings on sickness and disease upon the human race.

God wonderfully made every human being, but mental illness, cancers and diabetes is from the devil who loves to try to destroy you and me who are wonderfully made by God.

Even though we are wonderfully made by God, we can't totally blame the devil for our misfortunes in life because we've brought them upon ourselves.

We can't blame God for our misfortunes because God wonderfully made us to choose to love Him or not love Him.

We can make bad choices, but that doesn't take away from us that we are wonderfully made by God.

The devil knows that every human being is wonderfully made by God in every mother's womb.

A pregnant woman can take good care of herself and still have a deformed baby.

This just goes to show that the devil hates what God wonderfully made and the devil loves to make it look deformed.

Work on Being Black

Work on being black and don't try to be white, because white people don't truly know what it's like to be black.

Work on being black because being a black man, woman, boy and girl is who you are.

Got accepted you and me for being black, so who are we to not accept ourselves for being black?

If you work on being black, it will be a joy to be who God created you and me to be.

Working on being black will bring out more of our talents.

Working on being black will bring out more of our honesty

Working on being black will bring out more of our awareness.

Working on being black will bring out more of our presence.

Working on being black will bring out more of our love for ourselves and other races of people.

Many black people work on being accepted by other races of people.

Other races of people are more willing to accept us black people if we love the way that God created us to be.

Work on being black because many of us black people are very intelligent.

Work on being black because many of us black people are very spiritual people.

Work on being black because many of us black people are good people.

Work on being black because many of us black people are very wise people.

Work on being black because many of us black people are loving people.

Work on being black because many of us black people are respectful people.

Work on being black because many of us black people are very successful people.

Work on being black because many of us black people are creative people.

Work on being black because many of us black people are God-fearing people.

Other races of people are more willing to respect us black people if they see that we respect ourselves.

Other races of people are more willing to love us black people if they see that we black people love ourselves and love them.

Other races of people are more willing to help us black people if they see that we will help ourselves.

Other races of people are more willing to not judge us black people if they see that we accept ourselves for who we are.

Work on being black because being black is a great treasure to God.

Work on being black because being black brings forth good fruits from the black dirt in the ground.

Work on being black because being black is like a quiet dark night where we can get a good night's sleep.

Work on being black because being black is like the bold black universe that is forever present.

Work on being black because being black is beautiful upon many black women.

Work on being black because working on being black is not committing a crime that is also committed by other races of people.

Working on being black is freedom from deceiving ourselves that we are white when we are really black.

Work on being black because black will be around forever.

Many black people will work hard on their jobs, but they won't work on being black.

Many black people will work hard on their marriages, but they won't work on being black.

Many black people will work hard on their education, but they won't work on being black.

Many black people will work hard in the church, but they won't work on being black.

The Lord Jesus Christ wants you and me to work on being black because He created us to be black.

Work on being black because it's our purpose in life to be black and love and obey the Lord Jesus Christ.

Many black people don't love being black because they were told that black is ugly.

Many black people don't like being black because they were told that black is inferior.

Many black people don't love being black because they were told that black is dumb.

Many black people don't like being black because they were told that black is evil.

Work on being black because it is not a sin to be black.

Work on being black because black is strong to withstand prejudice and discrimination.

Work on being black because black is encouraged to take on oppression and injustice.

Work on being black because black is here to stay through the storms of police brutality upon black people.

Work on being black because black is shade from the hot, scorching sunlight of inequality.

Work on being black that is a champion over not being held back from achieving greatness.

Work on being black that is a warrior defeating stereotyping.

Work on being black that God cheerfully colored with His eternal crayon that no other race of people can break or throw away.

Work on being black like the sun works on shining its bright light down on us all day long.

Work on being black all day long to shine our black existence in this dark world.

Work on being black because Jesus Christ has worked out our soul's salvation for us black people to be saved.

Many people will degrade us for being black, but we can work on being black for God so He can work His unique presence into our black lives.

Work on being black because being black is not giving up on setting our minds to accomplishing our dreams.

Working on being black is facing up to many ignorant people of other races.

Many of our black men will work on killing one another and not work on being black and loving one another.

Many of our black people will work on pulling one another down like crabs in a barrel and not work on being black and pulling together.

Work on being black because God created us black people for His holy purpose.

Working on being black is a waste of time to black people who don't respect themselves.

Working on being black is a joke to black people who mistreat their own black people.

Work on being black because being black is trusting the Lord who many of our ancestors trusted through their hardships.

Work on being black because being black is real proof of survival in this world.

Work on being black because being black is greatly approved by God, who created us to live among other races of people every day.

Before I was Born

O Lord, You planned out my life before I was born.

O Lord, You foreknew that I would have some misfortunes in my life when You planned out my life.

O Lord, You foreknew that I would have some heartaches when You planned out my life.

O Lord, You planned out my life before I was born into this sinful world.

O Lord, You foreknew that I would have some disappointments in my life when You planned out my life.

O Lord, You foreknew that I would have some good days and some bad days when You planned out my life.

O Lord, You foreknew that I would make some mistakes in my life when You planned out my life.

O Lord, you foreknew that I would make some bad choices in my life when You planned out my life.

Before I was born, O Lord, You planned out my life for me to have no excuses to not deny myself and pick up my cross and follow You, my Lord and Savior Jesus Christ.

Before I was born, O Lord, You planned out my life for me to have no excuses to not choose to believe in You and love You and keep Your Commandments.

Love Your Neighbor

Love your neighbor when you are driving on the road.

Don't tailgate your neighbor.

Don't drive up on your neighbor's blind side on the road.

Love your neighbor in the grocery store.

Love your neighbor in the shopping malls.

Don't give your neighbor the evil eye look in the grocery store and shopping malls.

Love your neighbor on your job.

Don't talk mean to your neighbor on your job.

Love your neighbor when you walk down the street.

Don't walk into your neighbor.

Love your neighbor in your neighborhood where you live.

Speak to your neighbor in your neighborhood.

Love your neighbor in the church.

Be kind to your neighbor in the church.

Love your neighbor, no matter where you go.

Your neighbors are all around the world.

Love your neighbors in your home, where your spouse and your children are your neighbors in your house.

Love your neighbor every day that God commands you and me to love our neighbors.

Criminals don't love their neighbors.

The Devil Hates Every Human Being

The devil hates every human being, no matter whether they're black, white, brown or yellow. The devil's has caused many black men to kill other black men.

The devil has caused many white men to kill other white men.

The devil has caused many brown men to kill other brown men.

The devil has caused many yellow men to kill other yellow men.

There have been wars with white men killing other white men.

There have been wars with black men killing other black men.

The devil hates every human being in this world, where the devil wants to rule supreme over all men.

The devil is prejudiced against all human beings because he can't be saved in Jesus Christ and can't make it back to heaven where he once had it so good.

Any man who believes that the devil won't destroy him is only fooling himself.

No man can out hate the devil and be more prejudiced than the devil, who will cause any man to believe that he is a supreme being to rule this world.

Only Jesus Christ was able to get back the dominion over this world to save all men from being lost in our sins that are from the devil who hates every human being because we can get to heaven through Jesus Christ when he is forever lost in his sins.

If the Truth Offends You

If the truth offends you, then you know what you were doing is not right.

If the truth offends you, then you know that you are guilty of the wrong things that you do.

If the truth offends you, then you know that you need to be set free from lies.

If the truth offends you, then you know that you need to make things right.

If the truth offends you, then you know that the Lord is against what you say.

If the truth offends you, then you know that the Lord is against what you do.

If the truth offends you, then you know that you need to change.

If the truth offends you, then you know that you are not living right.

If the truth offends you, then you know that you can't fool everybody.

If the truth offends you, then you know that it's wrong to believe a lie.

If the truth offends you, then you know that God's word is powerful with nothing but the truth to set you free from the devil's lies.

The truth should offend you and me, if we are living a lie that hates the truth.

People Want to go to Heaven

People want to go to heaven, but many people don't treat everyone fair.

People want to go to heaven, but many people will cheat other people.

People want to go to heaven, but many people will kill other people.

People want to go to heaven, but many people will rob other people.

People want to go to heaven, but many people are having sex without being married.

People want to go to heaven, but many people are having sex with other people's spouses.

People want to go to heaven, but many people are in same-sex marriages.

People want to go to heaven, but many people don't respect everybody.

People want to go to heaven, but many tell lies.

People want to go to heaven, but many people don't love everybody.

People want to go to heaven, but many church people don't love everybody in the church.

People want to go to heaven, but many people don't believe in Jesus Christ.

People want to go to heaven, but many people don't love Jesus Christ.

People want to go to heaven, but many people are so lost in their sins.

If You Make Your Life Boring

If you make your life boring, it will be boring to you.

Your life is what you make it.

If you don't feel good about doing good things in life, then you will get bored sooner or later.

It's hard to get bored if you're doing good things in Jesus' name.

If you're doing nothing for the Lord, then sooner or later you will get bored in your life.

If you are on fire for the Lord, you won't get bored.

Jesus doesn't make anyone bored for loving Him and keeping His Commandments.

There is no boredom in working for Jesus, who knows how to keep our minds on His spiritual things that cause no child of God to get bored.

There is nothing boring about praying to the Lord Jesus Christ, who knows how to excite us with His love, mercy and Grace.

If you are caught up in Jesus, you won't get bored in your life.

Jesus knows how to always keep you and me going to spiritual heights that are never boring when the things in the world can bore us.

Jesus will never make us tired of doing good things in His holy name that will never make us bored to call on and speak about if we are excited about Jesus.

The Smarter You Are

The smarter you are, the more the devil will want to use you to deceive others who are not as smart as you.

The smarter you are, the more the devil will want to use you to use others who are not as smart as you.

The smarter you are, the more the devil will want to use you to cheat others who are not as smart as you.

The smarter you are, the more the devil will want to use you to hurt others who are not as smart as you.

The smarter you are, the more the devil will want to use you to lie to others who are not as smart as you.

The smarter you are, the more the devil will want to use you to pretend with others who are not as smart as you.

The Lord doesn't care about how smart you are.

The Lord doesn't care about how much you know.

The Lord doesn't care about how wise you are.

What the Lord cares about is that you love Him and believe in Him.

If you love the Lord, He will use you to bless others.

If you love the Lord, He will use you to show others His love for them.

A Storm Can Be a Blessing

A storm can be a blessing.

A storm can let us know how much we need the Lord.

A storm can let us know that the Lord is more powerful than the storm.

A storm can be a blessing to let us know that we are so weak without the Lord.

The storm was a blessing to Peter, who was one of Jesus' disciples.

If there was not a storm raging over the sea waters, Peter would not have ever walked on the water.

The Lord used the storm to test Peter's faith in Him.

Jesus knew that Peter would believe that He was stronger than the storm because Peter didn't hesitate to step off the boat and walk on the water towards Jesus, who also walked on the water.

If Jesus had not allowed that storm to rage on the sea waters, His disciples would not have known that even the storm would obey Him and move aside for Peter to walk on the water toward Jesus.

A storm can be a blessing to you and me to let us know that we are so fragile without Jesus Christ in our lives.

Ignorance

Ignorance causes many people to suffer through hardships.

Ignorance causes many people to make bad choices.

We are all ignorant towards something.

No one knows it all in this world.

The Pharisees and religious leaders crucified Jesus Christ due to their ignorance, even though Jesus dying on the cross had to be fulfilled.

When Jesus hung on the cross, He said to His Heavenly Father, "Forgive them for they know not what they do."

Jesus knew that the Pharisees and religious leaders and the Roman soldiers were ignorant towards what they were doing to Him.

For the lack of knowledge, people perish.

The lack of knowledge is ignorance that causes many people to perish.

Many people are ignorant towards God's holy word.

Many people choose to be ignorant towards God's holy word because they don't read it to know God's will for them.

Ignorance has started many wars that many soldiers didn't truly know what they were fighting and dying for in their ignorance.

Many ignorant people will go to hell for choosing not to know the truth and live the truth of God's holy word.

I Have to Point My Finger at Me

I have to point my finger at me for what I say.

I have to point my finger at me for what I do.

What I say it comes back to me.

What I do comes back to me.

I can't point my finger at someone else who I can't judge.

Even if someone else does me wrong, I can't judge him or her.

I don't know someone else's heart and can't point my finger at him or her.

I don't even know all of my own heart, only the Lord knows to judge me who must point my finger at me who has sins to confess and repent of unto the Lord.

It's so easy to point my finger at someone else, but I am no better than them in the eyes of the Lord.

I can easily point my finger at someone else's sins to try to make myself look good as if I have no sins before the Lord.

I have to point my finger at me who can never fool the Lord, but I can fool myself into thinking I am without sin.

The Lord can truly help me to change for the better, if I point my finger at me as if I was the only sinner who the Lord laid down His life for to save me from being lost in my sins.

I must point my finger at me who will answer to God who will judge me because I am no better than anyone else in the eyes of God.

Finger-pointing is for those who won't admit their own sins.

They love to cover up their sins, even in the church where you and I can feel pressed down under some clever, indirect finger-pointing.

I have to point my finger at me when it comes to the Lord Jesus Christ who is perfect without sin.

I can't point my finger at you and you can point your finger at me.

That should hurt me for me to see myself being a wretch without Jesus showing me that I am nothing good without Him in my life.

Destiny

All of us who know right from wrong have a destiny that we will choose.

Our destiny is heaven or hell and we ultimately choose where we will go.

If we are saved in Jesus Christ, we will go to heaven and that will be our destiny.

If we are lost in our sins, we will go to hell and that will be our destiny.

Every baby is destined to go to heaven because God will choose their destiny.

Every little child is destined to go to heaven because God will choose their destiny.

A baby doesn't know right from wrong.

A little child doesn't know right from wrong.

Little immature children are not mature enough to choose right from wrong.

God will not hold little children accountable for their sins because they are not mature enough to choose right from wrong.

All of us mature people will choose our destinies because God will judge us by the rights and wrongs that we know and do from day to day.

God will not judge little babies and little boys and girls whose sins will be on their parents.

There is nothing that we can choose in between our destiny, because we will either go to heaven or go to hell.

God created heaven and God created hell with nothing in between where we can go.

The Lord God doesn't choose the destiny of anyone who is mature enough to know right from wrong, the Lord God does choose for little babies and little children who don't know right from wrong.

It is their destiny to go to heaven if they die and never grow up to mature and choose right from wrong.

There are some mentally disabled adults who can't choose right from wrong, and God chooses their destiny to go to heaven because they are not mentally stable enough to choose their own destiny.

In the Army of God

In the Army, I was trained for physical fitness so that I would be sent to fight in a war.

In the Army, I was trained to tie different knots.

In the Army, I was trained to put up barbed wire fences.

In the Army, I was trained to armed and disarmed in M-15 anti-tank mines.

In the Army, I was trained to set up M-19 anti-personnel mines.

In the Army, I was trained to set up Claymore mines.

In the Army, I was trained to sweep land with a mine detector.

In the Army, I was trained to probe mines.

In the Army, I was trained to fire an M-16 machine gun.

In the Army, I was trained to fire an M-203 grenade launcher.

In the Army, I was trained to fire an M-72 rocket launcher.

In the Army, I was trained to fire an M-60 machine gun.

In the Army, I was trained to throw a hand grenade.

In the Army, I was trained to detect radiation.

In the Army I was trained to be a radio operator.

In the Army, I was trained to fight in a war that I never got a chance to fight in.

Every soldier must be trained to fight to the death.

Many soldiers have died, even though they had good training that was not 100% perfectly guaranteed to protect every soldier from being killed.

Today, I am in the army of God, fighting against spiritual wickedness that loves to shoot bullets of lies at me.

Today, I am in the army of God, fighting against spiritual wickedness that loves to throw grenades of rebellion at me.

Today, I am in the army of God, fighting against spiritual wickedness that loves to blast off its mines of deceptions at me.

Today, I am in the army of God, fighting against spiritual wickedness that loves to drop its bombs of hatred on me.

Today, I am in the army of God, fighting against spiritual wickedness that loves to spread its radiation of injustice upon me.

There are no spiritual casualties in God's Army that is equipped for every soldier to fight against spiritual wickedness.

Jesus Christ, our Lord and Saviour, is the top general of God's Army.

Jesus gives us the command to win the spiritual war by loving Him and keeping His Commandments so that spiritual wickedness will never be able to win the war against God.

Will Narrow Down To

It doesn't matter what our ministry is, when our Christian journey will narrow down to giving up everything that we have for the Lord.

It doesn't matter how much money we make, when our Christian journey will narrow down to giving up everything for the Lord.

It doesn't matter where we live, when our Christian journey will narrow down to giving up everything for the Lord.

It doesn't matter who we are, when our Christian journey will narrow down to giving up everything for the Lord.

There was a rich young man who believed that he loved the Lord, who had asked him to give up everything that he had and follow Him.

The rich young man could not do it because he loved his riches more than he loved the Lord.

There will come a day when your faith and my faith will be tested in the Lord.

If we live to see that day, will we give up or not give up everything that we have for the Lord?

Today is the time to let go of those things that can get between us and the Lord and cause our souls to be lost.

It doesn't matter how many spiritual gifts we have, when our Christian journey will narrow down to giving up everything we have, deny ourselves, and pick up our crosses and follow Jesus Christ.

It doesn't matter how much we have accomplished in the church, when it will narrow down to giving up everything that we have that's really not our own in the first place to the Lord.

That day will surely come for every child of God, and we will have to decide whether to give up or not give up everything that we have for the Lord, who is testing us all right now to see how much we love Him, even though he knows how much we love him.

We don't truly know how much we love the Lord until our love for Him is tested.

It doesn't matter how long we've been in the church, when our Christian journey will narrow down to giving up everything that we have for the Lord.

The Lord is not slack in giving us eternal things that will never wear out, break down or rust and erode, like things in this temporary world.

Life will narrow down to who will give up everything for Jesus' holy name.

It doesn't matter to the Lord if it's a little or a lot that we have to give up on our Christian journey that leads us to everything that Jesus will give to us in heaven one day.

I Will Survive

I will survive because I have You in my life, O Lord.

No matter what I go through in my life, I will survive because You are my strength, O Lord.

I will survive through my disappointments because I have You in my life, O Lord.

I will survive through the day because I have You in my mind, O Lord.

I will survive through my feelings because I have You in my heart, O Lord.

I will survive through my thoughts because I have You in my reasonings, O Lord.

I will survive through my attitude because I have You in my life, O Lord.

I will survive through my behavior because I have You in my life, O Lord.

I will survive through my actions because I have You in my choices, O Lord.

I will survive through my uncertainty because I have You in my presence, O Lord.

I will survive through my coming and going because I have You in my mobility, O Lord.

I will survive through my Brokenness because I have You in my mending, O Lord.

I will survive through my moment in time because I have You in my time here on Earth, O Lord.

I will survive through my destiny because I am saved in You, my Lord and Savior Jesus Christ.

It's Easy To

It's easy to talk bad about people who did you wrong.

It's easy to put people down who did you wrong.

It's easy to dislike people who did you wrong.

It's easy to not want to be around people who did you wrong.

It's easy to not want to talk to people who did you wrong.

It's easy to reject people who did you wrong.

It's easy to disrespect people who did you wrong.

It's easy to hate people who did you wrong.

You and I will do Jesus wrong in some kind of way.

It's easy to do people wrong for doing you wrong.

Jesus Christ, Our Lord and Savior, will never do you and me wrong.

If I do you wrong, I do Jesus wrong.

If you do me wrong, you do Jesus wrong.

It's easy to think bad about people who did you wrong.

It's easy to not want to help people who did you wrong.

It's easy for us to do Jesus wrong when Jesus will never do us wrong.

This Christian Journey

This Christian journey is not easy, but I love being on this Christian journey that gives me hope in Jesus Christ.

This Christian journey is not easy, but I love being on this Christian journey that gives me joy in Jesus Christ.

This Christian journey is not easy, but I love being on this Christian journey that gives me strength in Jesus Christ.

This Christian journey is not easy, but I love being on this Christian Journey that gives me peace of mind in Jesus Christ.

This Christian journey is not easy, but I love being on this Christian journey that gives me wisdom in Jesus Christ.

This Christian journey is not easy, but I love being on this Christian journey that gives me knowledge about Jesus Christ.

This Christian journey is not easy, but I love being on this Christian journey that gives me discernment in Jesus Christ.

This Christian journey is not easy, but I love being on this Christian journey that gives me humility unto Jesus Christ and my neighbors.

This Christian journey is not easy, but I love being on this Christian journey that gives me love for Jesus Christ and my neighbors.

Jesus Christ, my Lord and Savior, never promised me that this Christian journey would be easy.

Jesus didn't have it easy when He died on the cross to save me from my sins.

If anyone believes that this Christian journey is easy, then they haven't had that born-again life-changing experience in Jesus Christ.

My Life is Not About Me

My life is not about me, who was born in sin to easily sin against the Lord Jesus Christ.

My life is not about me, who can easily make mistakes when my Lord Jesus Christ has never made any mistakes.

My life is not about me, who can easily mess up things when my Lord and Savior Jesus Christ has never messed up anything.

My life is not about me, who can easily do something wrong when my Lord Jesus Christ has never done anything wrong.

My life is not about me, who has some regrets when my Lord Jesus Christ has never regretted anything.

My life is not about me, who can easily be selfish when my Lord and Savior Jesus Christ is forever selfless.

My life is not about me — my life is about Jesus Christ who gives me life to live my life unto Him every day.

My life is not about me, who can change when Jesus Christ my Lord is the same yesterday, today and tomorrow.

My life is not about me, who can get weak when my Lord Jesus Christ is eternally strong with victories to win.

Should Not Think Highly of Ourselves

You and I should not think highly of ourselves when people say some good things about us.

We should not let the good things go to our heads when people say good things about you and me.

It's always good to thank people for saying good things about us, but most of all it's always good to thank the Lord when people say some good things about you and me.

You and I should not think highly of ourselves when we make good accomplishments in our lives.

It's truly because of the Lord that you and I make good accomplishments in our lives.

The Lord says that we are supposed to esteem one another more highly than ourselves.

If you and I let it go to our heads when people esteem us, then we forget where the Lord brought us from, which is from the nothing that we were before we entered into our mothers' wombs.

You and I should not think highly of ourselves, no matter how much the Lord blesses us to do good things or great things.

To think highly of ourselves is to believe that we are better than others.

You and I should never think highly of ourselves because that would mean we're truly headed for a fall sooner or later in our lives.

The Greatest Ministry

The greatest ministry is living our lives unto the Lord day after day.

Life is the greatest ministry every day that we live to be truthful with everyone.

Life is the greatest ministry that we live to love everybody.

Life is the greatest ministry that we live to not falsely accuse anyone.

Life is the greatest ministry that we live to help those who we can help to especially love and obey the Lord.

The greatest ministry is living our lives to love and obey the Lord everyday.

Life is the greatest ministry that we live right by example.

Life is the greatest ministry that we live to believe in Jesus Christ.

Life is the greatest ministry that we live to uplift one another in the Lord.

Life is the greatest ministry that we live to be fair with everybody.

Life is the greatest ministry that we live to respect everybody.

Life is the greatest ministry that we live to be kind to everybody.

Life is the greatest ministry that we live to not harm anybody.

Life is the greatest ministry that we live to not kill anybody.

Life is the greatest ministry that we live to not abuse anybody.

Life is the greatest ministry that we live to not assault anybody.

Life is the greatest ministry that we live to not use anybody.

The greatest ministry is living our lives unto the Lord every day.

Our talents and gifts from the Lord are no match for the life that we live that has the greatest influence on everybody every day.

Some Things are Best To

Some things are best to not overlook.

Some things are best to not keep quiet about.

Some things are best to not ask any questions about.

Some things are best to not say.

Some things are best to walk away from.

Some things are best to not do.

Some things are best to forget.

Some things are best to leave alone.

Some things are best to let go of.

Some things are best to not talk about.

Some things are best to not laugh about.

Some things are best to not joke about.

Some things are best to not buy.

Some things are best to not sell.

Some things are best to not eat.

Some things are best to not drink.

Some things are best to move ahead on.

Some things are best to disagree on.

Some things are best to not sleep on.

Some things are best to not look at.

Some things are best to not listen to.

Some things are best to give up.

Some things are best to fight for.

Some things are best to hold onto.

Everything that Jesus says in His holy word is best for you and me to believe and live by.

Everything that Jesus did and is doing now is best for you and me to believe in Him and be saved.

It's God Who Gives

It's God who gives men and women gifts and talents and skills to do extraordinary things in this world.

Men and women can do nothing without God giving them inventions to create extraordinary things in this world.

It's because of God that men and women can fly jets and airplanes and helicopters.

It's because of God that men and women can build houses and skyscraper buildings.

It's because of God that men and women can jump and flip and kick around their bodies in gymnastics and martial arts.

It's because of God that men and women can drive tractor trailer trucks.

It's because of God that men and women can build cars, trucks, airplanes, trains and many more things in this world.

It's because of God that men and women and boys and girls can do incredible things.

It's God who gives men and women and boys and girls the wisdom and knowledge and ability to create things.

It's God who gives men and women and boys and girls genius, brilliance and intelligence to do extraordinary and incredible things in this world.

It's God who gives men and women and boys and girls the science and technology to do wonderful and great things in this world.

It's God who gives us all life, health and strength to accomplish things in life.

Great minds are from God, who created men, women, boys and girls in His image to do extraordinary, incredible and great things in this world.

Every man, woman, boy and girl should give the glory and praise to God, who is all-wise, all-knowledgeable, all-skillful, all-genius, all-brilliant, all-creative, all-intelligent, all-extraordinary, all-incredible, all-inventive, all-great, all-seeing and all-powerful beyond the angels in heaven.

All that God gives to us is to be used for His glory to build up His church for His Son Jesus Christ to come back to receive one day.

All that God gives us in this world is nothing compared to what He has for us in heaven where Jesus Christ will take us to for being saved in Him.

God gave us all His only begotten son that nothing else in this world can ever outdo and can't take Jesus' place no matter how extraordinary and incredible a man, woman, boy or girl can be.

Humbled

I am glad that you humbled me, O Lord, for me to see that I am no better than anyone else.

You humbled me, O Lord, for me to see how fragile I am without You protecting me, O Lord.

I am glad that you humbled me, O Lord, for me to know that I am nothing without You in my life from day to day.

When you humbled me, O Lord, I didn't know that it was for my own good and that the worst thing that could happen to me was being proud and dying lost in my sins.

I was once young and proud and didn't know You, O Lord, who I had greatly missed out on in my young life.

I am so glad today that you humbled me, O Lord, for me to see that my pride would have destroyed me if you didn't love me in my ignorant ways.

You humbled me, O Lord, and that was a good thing for me.

Many people believe that being humbled by You, O Lord, is a bad thing, but You, O Lord, would never do anything bad that would cause anyone's soul to be lost.

I thank you today, O Lord, for opening up my eyes to see that You humbled me to be a blessing to others who You love to save from being lost in their sins.

Humility is great grain in my life for me to trust and obey you, my Lord and Savior Jesus Christ.

If the Lord has to humble you and me, it's a blessing and not a curse because we can learn a lot of good things from being humbled by the Lord.

No one likes to be humbled by the Lord, but we can be truly thankful that the Lord will humble us to save our souls from going to hell.

I would rather be humbled by the Lord and make it to heaven, than be proud and go to hell.

I would rather be humbled by the Lord and be blind and paralyzed and make it to heaven, than be proud and athletic and go to hell.

If the Lord has humbled you and me, that is one great way that the Lord is letting us know that He hasn't given up on us and He will save us from our sins.

Being humbled by the Lord can be a painful thing, but it is a blessing to save our souls.

In the Book of Life

Will your face be in the Book of Life beyond your face being on Facebook?

Will my face be in the Book of Life beyond my face being on Facebook?

The Book of Life will have countless faces, more than the pebbles in the sand all around the world.

In the Book of Life, there will be cheer on everyone's faces for knowing that we made it to Heaven.

In the Book of Life, there won't be a teardrop on anyone's face.

In the Book of Life, there won't be a wrinkle on anyone's face.

In the Book of Life, there won't be a mole on anyone's face.

In the Book of Life there won't be a frown on anyone's face.

In the Book of Life, there won't be a look of disappointment on anyone's face.

In the Book of Life, there will be happiness on everyone's face.

In the Book of Life, there will be peace on everyone's face.

In the Book of Life there won't be sadness on anyone's face.

In the Book of Life, there won't be pimples on anyone's face.

In the Book of Life, there won't be blackheads on anyone's face.

In the Book of Life, there won't be any evil eye looks on anyone's face.

In the Book of Life, there won't be any guilty looks on anyone's face.

In the Book of Life, there will be a friendly look on everyone's face.

In the Book of Life there will be a holy look on everyone's face.

In the Book of Life there will be a righteous look on everyone's face.

In the Book of Life there will be a glorious look on everyone's face.

In the Book of Life, there will be a trustworthy look on everyone's face.

In the Book of Life, there will be an honest look on everyone's face.

Facebook doesn't have what the Book of Life will have for you and me to see when Jesus Christ comes back again.

The Book of Life will have no freckled faces.

The Book of Life will have no malnourished faces.

The Book of Life will have no war faces.

The Book of Life will have no mean faces.

The Book of Life will have no swollen faces.

The Book of Life will have no burned faces.

Every face that will be in the Book of Life will be a perfect face that Jesus Christ will create along with our new immortal and perfect body.

Facebook can't ever top that.

In the Book of Life, we won't have eyeglasses on our faces.

In the Book of Life there won't be any sweat on our face.

In the Book of Life there won't be any bumps on our face.

In the Book of Life there won't be any flaws on our face.

In the Book of Life, there won't be any lines under our eyes.

Facebook can't top that.

God Gives Us the Exams of Life

School teachers give their students exams to pass the courses that they take in school.

College professors give their college students exams to pass their college courses that they take in college.

Everyone does not pass all of their exams, even when they're homeschooled.

The exams in schools and colleges are no comparison to the exams that God gives to us to take and hopefully pass with a high score of faith in Him.

God gives us the exams of life that we will hopefully pass with a high score of trust in Him.

Hopefully we will pass God's exam of obedience with a high score.

The angels will give us our grade point average whether it's high or low from God's exams of life.

You can graduate from middle school, you can graduate from high school, you can graduate from homeschool, and you can graduate from college, but it's God's mercy and grace that graduates you and me from having no excuses to not live our lives unto God's Son Jesus Christ. God gives us all chances over and over again to pass His exams of life.

It's not the same in schools and colleges because if you fail the exams, your chances will run out for you to graduate.

You and I can fail God's exams over and over again, but God's grace is sufficient to help us to pass His exams so that we can have no excuses to keep failing God's exams.

We can pass God's exams because of His Son, Jesus Christ, who has passed all of God's exams so that you and I can be saved in Him and graduate to eternal life one day.

That will be the greatest graduation to march into heaven one day with honors of love and obedience unto the Lord God Jesus Christ.

Only the Lord Can Truly

Only the Lord can truly add more years to our life.

You can eat right and still get a virus that can make you sick and kill you.

It's always good to eat right, but eating right can't prolong our life like the Lord.

Only the Lord can truly add more years to your life.

You can drive safely on the highway roads and still get crashed into by another driver who is speeding.

You can get killed on the highway roads while driving safely.

It's always good to drive safely, but driving safely can't protect us on the highway road like the Lord.

Only the Lord can truly add more years to our life.

We can live in a beautiful house and still get killed by a plane crashing into our house.

It's a blessing to live in a beautiful house, but the house can't keep us from getting killed by a plane crashing into it.

Only the Lord can truly add more years to our life.

We can be in good health and still fall down and greatly injure ourselves and maybe die from our bad injury.

Only the Lord can truly protect us from injuring ourselves to the point of death, and add more years to our life.

No matter what we do right, only the Lord can truly add more years to our life.

Many good young people die upholding the law that can't truly add more years to our life.

We can be educated and still make a bad choice that can kill us.

It's always good to get a good education, but it's no guarantee that it will add more years to your life — only the Lord can do that.

Only the Lord can truly add more years to your life, which is something we can't truly do.

The uncertain, the unknown and the unpredictable can easily catch us off guard any time and anywhere and kill us, if the Lord allows it to kill us.

Only the Lord has truly allowed you and me to live this far in life for us to see this day.

You and I can't command more years be added to our lives — only the Lord can command that.

Only the Lord can truly add more years to our life on any day.

Only the Lord Jesus Christ can add more years to our lives beyond the mistakes that we make that can't override the Lord to give us more years to live.

www.ingramcontent.com/pod-product-compliance
Lightning Source LLC
Chambersburg PA
CBHW071353120626
46546CB00002B/677